The Decorator's Problem Solver

The Decorator's

Problem Solver

100 CREATIVE ANSWERS TO YOUR MOST COMMON DECORATING DILEMMAS

SACHA COHEN

Reader's Digest

The Reader's Digest Association, Inc.
Pleasantville, New York/Montreal

A READER'S DIGEST BOOK

Copyright Collins & Brown Ltd 2003
Text copyright © Sacha Cohen 2003
Design copyright © Collins & Brown Ltd 2003

This book was designed and produced by Collins & Brown Ltd.

FOR READER'S DIGEST
U.S Project Editor: Miranda Smith
Canadian Project Editor: Pamela Johnson
Project Designer: George McKeon
Executive Editor, Trade Publishing: Dolores York
Senior Design Director: Elizabeth Tunnicliffe
Director, Trade Publishing: Christopher T. Reggio
Vice President & Publisher, Trade Publishing: Harold Clarke

FOR COLLINS & BROWN
Editor: Kate Haxell
Designer: Roger Hammond
Photography: Lucinda Symons and Brian Hatton
Stylist: Diana Civil

Library of Congress Cataloging-in-Publication Data

Cohen, Sacha
   Decorator's problem solver: 100 creative answers to your most common
decorating dilemmas/Sacha Cohen
      p. cm
   Includes index
   ISBN 0–7621–0402–3
   1. Dwellings--Remodeling--Amateurs' manuals. 2. Interior decoration--Amateurs'
manuals. I. Title.

TH4816.C637 2003
643'.7--dc21
                                                        2002037119

NOTE TO OUR READERS
All do-it-yourself activities involve a degree of risk. Skills, materials, tools, and site conditions vary widely. Although the editors have made every effort to ensure accuracy, the reader remains responsible for the selection and use of tools, materials, and methods. Always obey local codes and laws, follow manufacturer's operating instructions, and observe safety precautions.

Address any comments to:
The Reader's Digest Association, Inc.
Adult Trade Publishing
Reader's Digest Road
Pleasantville, NY 10570-7000

For more Reader's Digest products and information visit our website:
www.rd.com (in the U.S.)
www.readersdigest.ca (in Canada)

Printed and bound in Imago in Singapore

 3 5 7 9 10 8 6 4 2

Contents

Introduction 8

● Materials & techniques 10

● Walls 36

● Floors 68

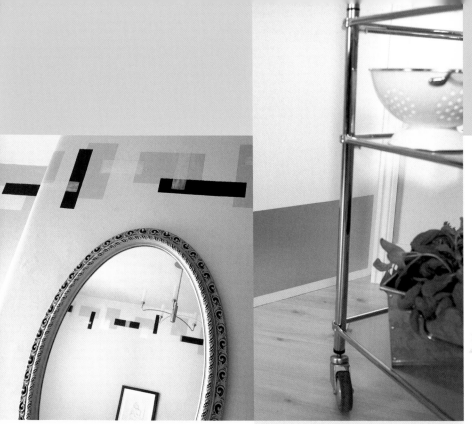

● Rooms 136

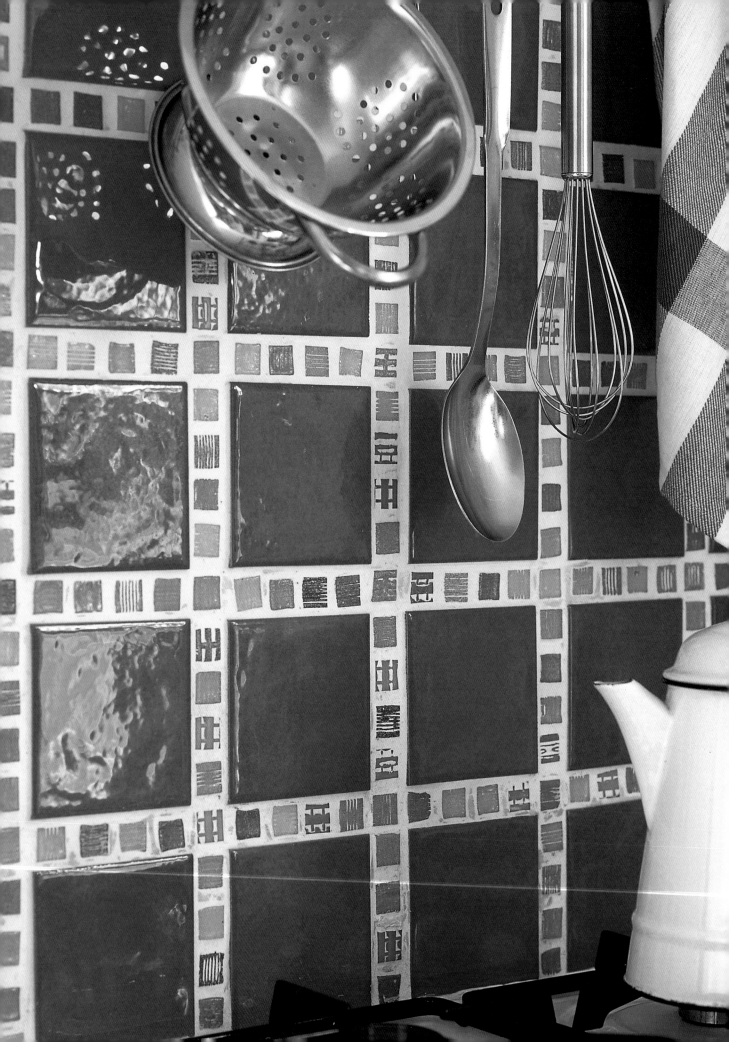

Introduction

THERE IS LITTLE that beats the satisfaction of transforming a drab room into a fresh, inviting space. The pleasure of knowing that your own work has created this change is one shared by all decorators. However, the problems encountered in decorating can be daunting. In this book you will find a solution—in fact, one hundred solutions—to over thirty common decorating problems, just the sorts of problems that you are facing.

Every property, whether it's old or new, has decorating problems and will probably need a little more than a lick of paint to turn it into a dream home. Or maybe you have decided that the time has come for a major refurbishment of your much-loved house, which has become a little shabby since you last decorated ten years ago. Perhaps you want to redecorate just one room but only have a few dollars to spend.

In any case, there are always problems to overcome. Common problems you may be facing include lack of light, unattractive tiles, damaged walls, an outdated kitchen or bathroom—of course, there is always the problem of budget.

You don't need to be an expert decorator to use this book. In fact, just the opposite is true. We have written the book for use by homeowners of all skill levels. The simple skills needed to master each solution are explained in detailed step-by-step instructions in the *Core Techniques* section, with variations on them in each individual solution. The materials and tools used are basic and available in most home improvement stores.

There are solutions to suit different tastes and interior schemes, from cool and contemporary to cozy country. Whether you are decorating a kitchen, bedroom, bathroom, living room, hall, or even a basement, there is a solution to suit your individual problem, your taste, and your pocketbook.

Sacha Cohen

THE MATERIALS NEEDED to carry out the solutions in this book are all readily available at hardware or home improvement stores, and the core techniques are simple to master. In the tools and equipment section you will find tips on which tools are absolutely essential and those that will make your task easier but are not vital to the success of the project. The techniques are clearly illustrated and carefully explained, and advice is offered as to when you would be better off asking a professional to do specific jobs for you.

Of course, if you are an experienced and enthusiastic decorator, you may choose to undertake all the work yourself, but please consider the skills needed before embarking on a task. The time and cost involved in fixing mistakes is sometimes better spent on employing someone else to get it right the first time.

materials & techniques

Decorating materials

There is a vast array of materials available to the home decorator, but you only need a basic selection to carry out most of the solutions in this book. No solution requires all of the materials discussed here, so once you have chosen a solution, check the materials listed to see what is required before you go shopping.

This book deals with common decorating problems and uses commonly available materials. The materials listed here are commercially available in home improvement stores, though some may only be carried by larger stores.

Whenever you buy a decorating material, and particularly if you are going to be using it for the first time, read the instructions, paying attention to any safety precautions, and follow them carefully to achieve the best results.

Paints

Paint is the decorator's primary material. Its basic function is to add color and decoration to walls, ceilings, woodwork, floors, and furniture. Paint can be applied as flat color, or by using one of the paint effects shown in this section and in some of the solutions in later sections in this book.

A secondary function of paint, which is often overlooked, is to protect the surface it's applied to, and there are specialized paints available for almost any job that you can think of. However, for most decorating purposes, and certainly for the purposes of this book, there are just three main types of paint to consider and a few specialized ones.

MATTE LATEX PAINT

This is the most commonly used type of paint and is suitable for walls and ceilings. The finish is opaque and matte. It can also be diluted into a wash and used on wood (see page 25).

Latex paint is also available in a medium-luster finish, often called satin. This is easily wiped down, and it's often a good choice for kitchens and bathrooms. The techniques in this book use matte paint, since the non-reflective surface is more forgiving on imperfect surfaces, but you can use a medium-luster finish if you prefer.

Latex paint is water-based, making it quick-drying and low-odor. However, this doesn't mean that it's water soluble—you can still wash walls once the paint is dry.

Matte latex paint has no luster and a slightly chalky look when dry.

Smooth and low-luster, eggshell paint tones well with a matching matte latex paint.

EGGSHELL PAINT

Used for painting woodwork, this paint has an opaque, low-luster finish. It can be either water- or oil-based. Water-based paints have several advantages over oil-based paints: they are low-odor, whereas oil-based paints can give off harmful vapors; they dry more quickly; and they are more environmentally friendly. However, on the whole, they are not as tough as the oil-based versions, and this should be considered when choosing paint for a specific job.

Eggshell paint can be mixed to exactly match a latex paint, and once dry, the differences between the two are insignificant because the finishes are similar.

SATIN PAINT

This type of paint is also used on woodwork, and has an opaque, medium-luster finish. It, too, is available as a water- or oil-based paint, and the same considerations used for eggshell apply when choosing which to use. Satin paint can also be mixed to exactly match a latex paint, but as the surface of satin paint has a luster, it will look a slightly different color when dry if it's placed right next to matte paint. If you are using medium-luster latex paint on walls, however, then satin paint will provide a better color match for woodwork than eggshell.

In addition, high gloss paint is commercially available. It has an opaque, high-luster finish. High gloss paint hasn't been used in this book, since it's generally only available with an oil base, and the high sheen is so unforgiving that it should only be used on woodwork in perfect condition.

METALLIC PAINT

Metallic paints have limited use for the home decorator, but can be used where a light-reflective surface is needed, or to paint highlights in a decorative finish. They are widely available in silver and gold, and other colors can be found in more specialized decorating stores. Pearlized paint—reflective gloss paint that changes in appearance with changing light—is available in a range of colors. Pearlized paints can be used in the same way as metallic paints. Both paints are water-based and can be used on walls and ceilings.

In addition, gilt creams and metal leaf have a role to play in interior decoration. Gilt cream can be used over any painted surface to add a light metallic sheen and is particularly useful if you want to add a metallic finish to molding or to parts of a piece of furniture.

Metal leaf is used to gild a surface. It must be stuck down with a suitable size, such as Japan size, and can be applied to almost any solid material. It produces a rich, metallic finish, but is best used in small areas, since it's time-consuming to apply. The size you select will depend to a large extent on the job you are doing. Choose between the fast-drying, water-based size and the slower-drying Japan size accordingly. Read the instructions on the bottle and follow them carefully for best results.

Metal leaf is commonly available in silver, gold, and copper finishes, and interesting, multi-colored finishes are also available. You can even use real gold and silver leaf but imitation leaf is much less expensive and provides the same degree of metallic sheen.

Smooth, and with a medium-luster finish, satin is the most commonly used type of paint for decorating woodwork.

(left to right): Gilt cream, metal leaf paint, and metallic paint can be used to add shimmering accents to a decorative scheme.

Surface textures

Adding texture to the surface is a good choice for the decorator who has to deal with less than perfect surfaces, as it will hide a multitude of sins. Damage such as surface cracks and pits, unevenness, and paradoxically, other, less attractive textures, can all be hidden or disguised.

There are various types of texture, but in this book only two are needed to carry out any of the solutions.

INTERIOR TEXTURED COVERING

This is a thick, white substance that can be used on walls and ceilings. It's painted onto the surface with a large paintbrush and then treated in different ways to achieve different effects. In the 1970s, when this material was developed, it was popularly used to create ridged and swirled ceilings, which dated quickly, and so the material became unfashionable. However, it does have uses in the modern home and should not be dismissed.

The main drawback of textured covering is that it's very difficult to remove once it has dried on the wall. Therefore, when contemplating solutions that use this material, take this into account, and if you are not sure it's what you want, then choose another solution that can be painted over or removed more easily.

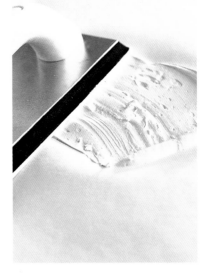

Interior textured covering can be used to imitate rough plaster by smoothing over it with a grout float.

TEXTURED MASONRY PAINT

Designed for painting the outside of houses, this paint is very durable. It has a light texture that goes a long way toward obscuring small defects in walls and ceilings. If the surface you are decorating is lightly damaged and you are using a decorating solution not specifically designed to combat this, then substituting masonry paint for latex paint will help to cover the problems. Thorough sanding will restore a plaster wall to smoothness once it has been covered with this paint, but this is time-consuming, so paint a board first to check that you are happy with the finish before painting the whole room.

Masonry paint is available off the shelf in a limited range of colors and in a wider range from a paint-mixing system. However, you may find it easier—and it's certainly cheaper—to tint white masonry paint with a colorizer. These are small tubes of intense color pigment, a small amount of which will turn white into a pastel tone. Decant enough paint to do your job into a large paint can, and squeeze in some colorizer. Stir the two together with a stirring stick until the mixture is smoothly blended and the color even.

Squeeze a small amount of colorizer into the paint to start with. You can always add more if you want to strengthen the tone once it has been mixed.

The paint must be stirred until the color is smoothly blended. If you paint it onto the walls at the half-stirred stage shown here, the results will be uneven and patchy.

Wallpapers

Wallpaper is a popular decorating material, but you will find it used only rarely in this book. This isn't because wallpaper is a bad decorating choice, but because hanging it properly is a labor-intensive and time-consuming task that is all too easy to get wrong unless you have a lot of experience. This book concentrates on simple, creative solutions that can be tackled by even the most inexperienced decorator.

If you do want to wallpaper your room and you are not a seasoned decorator, you may wish to call in a professional. Although this will cost money, the time and anguish saved—and the cost of more paper to correct any mistakes—make the price worth it.

Having said this, there is a very wide range of wallpapers commercially available, and if your walls are in reasonable condition, wallpapering can be a good decorative option.

Despite the vast range of wallpapers, most of them perform the same basic function. Shown here are some examples of the main types available.

Patterned papers come in a myriad of colors and designs.

Vinyl papers are washable and therefore a suitable option in a kitchen or bathroom.

Above: *Plain textured papers will cover a lot of damage and can be painted with latex paint.*

Right: *Texture, color, and pattern are combined on some papers, allowing you to cover damage and introduce decoration in one step.*

Above: *Paper borders are designed to be used instead of a dado or picture rail. However, both of these elements are traditionally used in older homes, where their function is to divide up high walls. You can use them in a modern home, too, but be aware that dividing walls with horizontal bands will visually lower the ceiling, which isn't always a good thing.*

Tiles

Tiles are excellent for waterproofing walls and floors, though their cost can take them out of reach of the decorator who is working on a tight budget. While the price of a single tile may be low, when you multiply that cost by the number of tiles needed, tiling a large area can become an expensive option. Therefore, in this book they are used to cover small areas that demand the specific benefits that tiles offer: a waterproof, durable surface that is also decorative.

This does not, however, mean that only cheap, plain tiles can be used. If the area you are working on is small, consider using some more expensive decorative tiles as accents and plainer ones to cover the majority of the surface.

As with wallpapers, there is a vast range of tiles on the market, all performing the same function, but with different finishes. Though new technology has produced a number of extraordinary tiles (such as glass, plastic, and resin tiles), the most commonly used and most widely available are ceramic tiles, which can be found in many different colors, sizes, and patterns, and are therefore the only ones used in this book. Shown here are examples of the most commonly available types.

White 4- or 6-inch (10- or 15-cm) square tiles are the cheapest option and can be combined with other tiles to produce a more decorative finish.

Textured tiles tend to be expensive, but like mosaic tiles, they can be used as accents in an area of plain tiling.

Handmade tiles are usually 4 inches (10 cm) square and come in a wide range of colors. Part of their charm lies in the less uniform glazed surface.

Patterned tiles come in all shapes, sizes, and designs. They are usually more expensive and should be a carefully considered purchase.

Mosaic tiles can be made from vitreous glass, ceramic, and even metal. Though an expensive option in large quantities, just a few can be used to bring an entirely fresh look to plain tiles.

Edge tiles are a very useful option. They are available in a range of colors and profiles, and a few can be used to neatly and decoratively finish an area of plain tiles.

Flooring

Flooring can be the single most expensive purchase a decorator has to make. As such, it needs to be a carefully planned choice. There are solutions in this book for creating inexpensive yet interesting floors, but they may not be suitable for all rooms.

If you do need to buy flooring, first decide on exactly what you need, and then look at what is available before making the purchase. It may be best to buy the flooring first and then decorate the room to match it, rather than trying to do it the other way around.

Flooring is generally broken up into three main types: tiles, wood, and carpet. Each type has different properties and different advantages and drawbacks.

TILES

There are various types of floor tile, from ceramic to vinyl and cork. Ceramic floor tiles, like wall tiles, offer a hard-wearing, waterproof surface that is ideally suited to a bathroom or kitchen. On the other hand, they are hard, cold (unless under-floor heating is laid), and expensive. They must be laid on a solid, completely flat floor, or they will crack in time, and they should be laid by a professional or an experienced decorator, because getting the arrangement wrong can be expensive and time-consuming to correct.

Vinyl tiles also offer a waterproof surface, and they are very durable. They are easy to lay and cut and relatively inexpensive. Their drawback is that they are only available in a limited range of sizes and colors, though if one of these colors suits you, they are a good option for budget decorating.

Cork tiles are also a good, inexpensive option. They can be customized to complement an interior scheme and are easy to lay. However, they are not the most durable of surfaces and unless they are carefully sealed, should not be used in areas prone to wetness, such as kitchens or bathrooms.

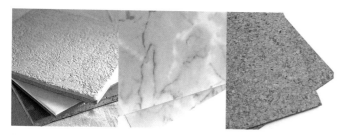

(left to right): *Ceramic tiles can be glazed or unglazed, and different surfaces have different applications. Vinyl tiles are usually self-adhesive, and laying them is clean and easy. Cork tiles can be bought sealed or unsealed; the unsealed versions can be painted to match a room.*

WOOD

This is a traditional flooring material that has become popular again in recent years. Floorboards are still used in the construction of most homes, and can be sanded, stained, or painted, depending on the finish you want. They are hard-wearing, but need to be sealed, especially in a kitchen or bathroom. The surface is hard underfoot, but you can use rugs to soften them, both physically and visually.

Laminate flooring is a new product that has taken the home improvement market by storm. The better versions look just like wood, with the added bonus of being water-resistant and completely smooth. Laminate flooring is easy to lay and usually comes in kits, with all the necessary instructions included.

(top left to bottom right): *Pale ash laminate; medium beech laminate; stained wooden floorboards; natural, varnished floorboards.*

CARPET

The most popular flooring option for many people, carpet is warm, soft, provides good sound insulation, and is available in many textures and colors. The primary drawbacks are cost and durability. While better quality carpets wear well, most carpets react badly to spills. This makes carpet a dangerous choice for kitchens and children's rooms, though the softness is a bonus for toddlers who are not quite steady on their feet. In this case, it may be a good idea to buy an inexpensive carpet for their room, and reconcile yourself to the inevitable damage. Special water-resistant carpet is available for kitchens and bathrooms, but in a limited range of colors.

If you decide to carpet a room, buy the best you can afford, clean it regularly, and use mats or rugs in areas subject to heavy traffic. This will ensure that your carpet remains in the best possible condition.

(top to bottom): *Tufted carpet is soft underfoot. Woven carpet is harder, but usually more hard-wearing.*

Tools and equipment

There is a vast, complicated, and expensive range of tools and equipment available to the home decorator, most of which you simply don't need. The tools that are necessary and others that will make tasks a little easier are on these pages.

Once you have chosen a solution to work on, check the materials list to see what tools you will need. Buy the best ones that you can afford, especially when it comes to paintbrushes, but always ask advice from a store assistant; the most expensive tool isn't always the best one to buy.

There are some simple guidelines for using tools.
- Be careful when using any tool, and always read through any safety instructions.
- If you are using power tools, never, ever leave them running unattended.
- Remember that children are often fascinated by anything an adult uses, so keep tools out of reach of small hands.
- Don't use a tool for a job that it was never intended to do. You may damage it and yourself.
- Take care of your tools, keep them clean, store them neatly, and they will last for years.

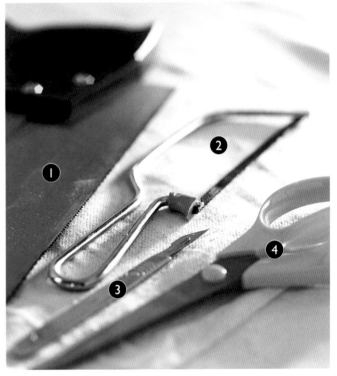

EQUIPMENT FOR MEASURING AND MARKING

- A long spirit level (**1**) with measurements marked along one edge —an expensive, but very useful tool. Buy one if you can.
- A retractable tape measure (**2**)—you will need some sort of measuring instrument for most jobs; this is the best budget buy.
- A try-square (**3**)—useful for establishing a true 90-degree angle, particularly in woodworking.
- A long steel ruler (**4**)—useful, but not essential.
- A short spirit level (**5**)—you will need one, so buy this if you cannot afford the long one.
- A short steel ruler (**6**)—necessary for smaller tasks and for cutting against.

TOOLS FOR CUTTING

- A backsaw (**1**)—the most useful type of saw to buy.
- A hacksaw (**2**)—useful for specific tasks.
- A craft knife (**3**)—essential. Keep the blade covered with a cork and change it frequently.
- Scissors (**4**)— very useful; keep a pair just for your own projects.

EQUIPMENT FOR MASKING

- Painting tape (**1**)—a specially designed masking tape for masking off on existing paintwork. This low-tack tape is inexpensive and essential for most painting jobs.
- ¾-inch (2-cm), 1-inch (2.5-cm), and 3-inch- (7.5-cm-) wide masking tapes (**2**), 1½-inch (4-cm), ½-inch (12-mm), and 2-inch- (5-cm-) wide masking tapes (**3**). These masking tapes are inexpensive, and different widths are useful for different jobs; buy them as you need them. Always buy low-tack tape because ordinary masking tape can pull off paint when it's removed.

EQUIPMENT FOR SANDING

- 240-grit sandpaper (**1**)—useful for some woodworking projects.
- 120-grit sandpaper on a sanding block (**2**)—the best type of sandpaper to buy for most projects. A sanding block is essential for all woodworking projects, and useful for many others.
- Sanding sponge (**3**)—good for sanding walls and moldings.
- Wet and dry, very fine sandpaper (**4**)—essential for sanding paint on woodwork between coats for a perfect finish.

TOOLS AND EQUIPMENT FOR PREPARING WALLS AND WALLPAPERING

- Spackle (**1**)—essential for filling cracks in walls.
- Small trowel (**2**)—essential for applying filler.
- Scraper (**3**)—essential for removing old wallpaper.
- Wallpaper paste (**4**) and seaming roller (**5**)—essential for wallpapering.
- Sponge roller (**6**) and lining paper (**7**)—essential for wallpapering.

TOOLS FOR PAINTING

- 2-inch (5-cm) paintbrush (**1**)—essential for most painting projects.
- Sable artist's paintbrush (**2**)—useful for painting glass.
- Stenciling brush (**3**)—useful only for stenciling.
- 1-inch (2.5-cm) paintbrush (**4**)—essential for painting narrow woodwork.
- 4-inch (10-cm) paintbrush (**5**)—essential for painting large areas.
- 3-inch (7.5-cm) paintbrush (**6**)—useful for some painting projects.
- Small artist's paintbrush (**7**)—useful for small detail.
- Large stippling brush (**8**)—essential for stippling large areas.

Long-pile roller and roller tray; essential for painting large areas quickly.

Gloss roller; useful for smoothly painting satin or eggshell onto large areas of woodwork.

EQUIPMENT FOR FILLING AND STICKING

- Project glue (**1**)—powerful, gap-filling adhesive, essential for some solutions.
- Joint compound (**2**)—useful for filling small cracks in walls and woodwork.

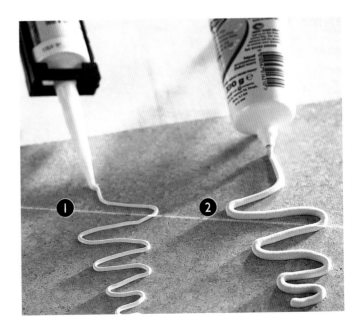

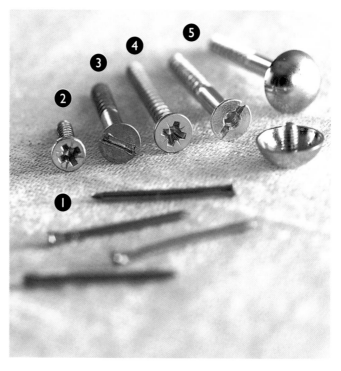

TOOLS FOR FASTENING

■ Hammer (**1**)—useful for woodworking projects.
■ Screwdriver with interchangeable heads (**2**)—essential for many projects. Having interchangeable heads saves buying several different screwdrivers, so it's a good long-term investment.

ASSORTED SCREWS AND NAILS

■ Small nails (**1**); short Phillips-head screw (**2**); medium slot-head screw (**3**); long Phillips-head screw (**4**); screws with decorative caps (**5**). It's essential to have a small, mixed selection of general purpose nails and screws. Screws with decorative caps are essential for projects where the screw-head will show, and should therefore be attractive.

THE DECORATOR'S MOST BASIC TOOL KIT

If you are a novice decorator, with no tools or equipment but plenty of enthusiasm, these are the first things you should buy. With these and some paint, you will be able to do most things.

■ 1-inch (2.5-cm) flat, square-ended soft-bristled paintbrush (**1**).
■ 3-inch (7.5-cm) long-bristled paintbrush (**2**).
■ Long spirit level with measurements marked along one edge (**3**).
■ Painting tape (**4**).

WORKING SAFELY

Invest in a sturdy set of stepladders, tall enough to access all parts of the room without stretching or over-reaching. Don't use paint from the large can; instead, decant small amounts as required into a smaller can or tray, and firmly replace the lid on the original can. This means that if the paint is spilled, there is far less to clean up. Use a ladder attachment to either hang the can from or support the roller tray so that you have one hand free to hold onto the ladder.

Work in a well-ventilated room; even low-odor paints can become overwhelming if you are painting all day in an enclosed space.

Don't rush a job. The time key given with each solution will give you a rough idea how long the work will take to do, and you need to add drying times to this. Set aside enough time and work methodically through the instructions for the solution. Rushing the job or cutting corners will have a detrimental effect on the end result, and if you fall off the ladder because you were in too much of a hurry to climb down and move it to a better position, it will have a detrimental effect on you.

Don't assume that you know how to use a product because you have used a similar one before. Read the instructions for anything you are using, especially if it's the first time, and follow them.

Don't be put off by these simple, commonsense precautions, they are here to help you achieve your goal without trouble.

Pour a small amount of paint into a metal or plastic paint can and paint from that.

PREPARING TO WORK

Once you have decided on the solution that you want to use for your specific problem, gather together the tools, equipment, and materials you will need. There is nothing more frustrating, and potentially detrimental to your project, than having to stop halfway through because you don't have something that you need.

Next, clear the space you are going to tackle as much as possible. Any furniture left in the room should be moved to the middle and covered with polyethylene. Don't just cover furniture with a decorator's drop cloth, because spilled paint can soak through it and stain the furniture underneath.

Cover the floor with a polyethylene sheet, taped down around the baseboards with masking tape.

Over this, spread a drop cloth to soak up any small spills or splatters. Unplug any electrical equipment so that you don't trip over the wires.

Take down all the curtains and rods if you are painting the walls. Remove the door handles if you are painting the doors. These measures can eliminate paint splattering accidents, save tricky cutting in, and provide a better finish.

This may all seem like a lot of fuss, but when you have spilled paint on your new armchair, tripped over a wire and sent the lamp on the other end of it crashing to the floor, and transferred more paint from the soles of your shoes onto your expensive carpet, you will wish that you had taken the time to prepare properly before you started.

CHOOSING THE RIGHT SOLUTION

Each of the common decorating problems that this book deals with has at least one solution. The solution you choose will depend on a number of criteria: personal taste, the condition of the surface you want to decorate, the amount of effort you want to invest, the size and shape of your room, your budget, and the amount of time you have available.

The photograph of each finished solution will give you an idea of how the effect will look in your room, and many of the solutions offer advice on customizing the finish to suit a different environment.

Each solution has a key, an example of which is shown below. There are four different elements in each key, and they contain the following information.

Nature of problem:
This summarizes the decorating problem that the solution aims to help you overcome.

Extent of solution:
This advises you as to how far the solution goes in eradicating the problem. This is an important factor to consider when choosing a solution. If you are renting your home and don't want—or are not allowed by your landlord—to undertake a permanent solution that may physically alter the room, then choose a solution that offers a *visual* disguise or enhancement, rather than a *physical* enhancement or disguise, or permanent change. If you are decorating a new home on a budget, but at some time in the future you plan to completely refurbish the house, a quick-fix enhancement or disguise to eliminate an unsightly element in a room may be a better choice than a more time-consuming, permanent solution that you may be changing in a few years.

Finish:
This summarizes the finish the solution will give.

Nature of problem:
uneven wall

Extent of solution:
visual disguise

Finish:
mottled color

Time:
2 hours

Time:
This offers a very rough guide to the working time needed for each solution. You need to add drying times to this—most products state a recommended drying time on the packaging. Obviously, if you are an experienced decorator, a solution may take you less time than stated, and equally, if you are a novice, it may take a little longer.

The times have been based on working on areas of a specific size, so measure the area you wish to work on and multiply or divide the time accordingly. The areas used are as follows:
- Walls: 8 × 8 feet (2.5 × 2.5 m).
- Tiles: 3 × 3 feet (1 × 1 m).
- Floors: 10 × 10 feet (3 × 3 m).
- Ceilings: 10 × 10 feet (3 × 3 m).
- Doors: 2 ½ × 6 ¼ feet (75 cm × 1.8 m).
- Windows: 2 × 3 feet (60 cm × 1 m).

Some solutions deal with elements of specific sizes, for example, the standard drop cloths used as drapes on page 130, or the collaged bands on page 48. In these instances the timing is based on working with these elements.

QUANTITY GUIDE

The quantity of a product needed to complete a solution can be difficult to judge. Different brands of paint cover different areas, as do different textured coverings, pastes, and adhesives. Measure the area you are going to work on, read the recommendation on the product, and always allow the following.

- **Paint:** generally allow enough for two coats, although if you are painting a pale color over another pale color, one coat will generally suffice.
- **Tiles:** allow 5 percent extra for breakages and miscalculations. If you are following a broken tile solution, don't buy any extra for breakages.
- **Wallpaper:** allow enough for any pattern repeat; the pattern match measurement is usually stated on the roll.

Again, some solutions deal with elements that will need to be sized to suit your room or cover your problem, such as the faux panels on page 52. In these instances, advice on measuring the space is given with the solution.

Finally, it's always best to buy a little extra of everything. Tiles may break, a length of wallpaper may get creased or marked while you are hanging it, and if the store has run out of stock, you will be in trouble. Most stores will allow you to return unopened boxes or rolls of a product. Paint isn't returnable, but surfaces always need touching up at some point, and the color of a new batch may be slightly different from the one you originally bought.

Core techniques

The basic decorating techniques you need to master in order to tackle the solutions in this book are all explained in this section. No single solution needs more than two core techniques, and you will find the techniques necessary for each solution listed in a section below the materials needed. Read through the appropriate core technique and all additional information given with the solution before you start.

PAINTING

Painting is a simple process, but it does pay to prepare the wall surface properly before you start work. Depending on the state of the walls you are working on—whether they are uneven, cracked, or pitted—there are various procedures that should be followed. Check the wall and assess the level of damage, then read through the following directions and follow those that are appropriate.

Filling

YOU WILL NEED

☐ Plaster of Paris or epoxy filler
☐ Small trowel
☐ 120-grit sandpaper

IF the wall or ceiling you are working on is old, you may need to fill cracks and holes before you can start to paint.

First, remove any loose particles of plaster. Then, following the instructions on the packet, mix up plaster of Paris with water, or epoxy filler if it's a large hole, until it becomes a thick paste.

1 Apply this to the damaged area with a small trowel, scraping back most of the excess, but leaving just a little. This allows for any shrinking back while the filler is drying.

2 Sand to a smooth finish, testing the evenness of the surface by running your fingertips over it. They will detect more uneven areas than the eye will.

Cleaning

YOU WILL NEED

☐ Light detergent mixed with water
☐ Sponge

DIRT and grease on any surface will prevent the paint from properly adhering, causing it to peel away after only a short time. You can easily avoid this by simply washing the surface before painting it.

Use a light detergent and a sponge to wash each wall. The surface should be left to dry completely before you start painting.

Mist coat and pickling stain

NEW plaster will need a primer to seal the absorbent surface and allow the top coat paint to grip. Matte latex paint mixed with water adequately serves the purpose. The same mixture is also used for pickling stain (see page 80).

Pour some latex paint into a paint can. Pour in a roughly equal amount of water. You will have to judge this by eye, but it isn't necessary that the proportions are exact. Stir the two together well. Brush this mist coat over all the newly plastered areas using a roller or paintbrush and leave to dry before painting the next coats of solid paint.

YOU WILL NEED
- ☐ Matte latex paint
- ☐ Water
- ☐ 3-inch (7.5-cm) paintbrush or roller

Rollering paint

THIS is very simple and quick to do. However, you will need to use a paintbrush for all the edges and corners because a roller will not reach and a clean line is needed.

Decant some paint into the roller tray. Roll the roller through the paint, then roll it backwards and forwards on the ridged part of the tray until it's evenly covered. Roll the paint onto the wall in random directions to give a smooth finish.

YOU WILL NEED
- ☐ Matte latex paint
- ☐ Roller tray
- ☐ Roller

Mixing a colorwash

COLORWASH is a mix of paint and another material that slows down the drying time of the paint to give you more time to create an effect. There are various specialist glazes you can buy, but ordinary wallpaper paste works just as well and is far less expensive. The proportions needed are 1 part wallpaper paste to 1 part paint. Estimate how much paint you would need to paint the wall conventionally (see page 23), and halve that amount.

In the paint can, mix up the wallpaper paste according to the manufacturer's instructions. Mix up the same volume of paste as the amount of paint you have estimated you need. Add the paint and stir thoroughly to create an even colorwash. Apply this using the *Mottled Coat of Paint* technique (see page 26).

YOU WILL NEED
- ☐ Paint can
- ☐ Wallpaper paste
- ☐ Water
- ☐ Matte latex paint in your chosen color
- ☐ Stirring stick

Flat coat of paint

APPLYING paint to the wall with a paintbrush will give a flatter finish, without the orange peel texture a roller produces. However, it does take longer, and you may prefer to use a roller on large areas.

If you are painting with a brush, follow these simple steps to ensure that the paint is evenly smoothed out and the brush marks are kept to a minimum. Only dip the first two-thirds of the bristles into the paint.

YOU WILL NEED

☐ Matte latex paint

☐ 4-inch (10-cm) paintbrush

1 Dip the bristles of the paintbrush into the paint, scrape off one side of the brush on the side of the can, and paint two thick, vertical stripes on the wall, approximately 2 feet (60 cm) long and 6 inches (15 cm) apart. This should transfer most of the paint on the brush onto the wall.

2 Immediately brush across the stripes, working from side to side, spreading the paint out across the wall.

3 Working quickly, brush lightly over the painted area, using even, vertical strokes. This is known as "laying off," and it ensures that any visible brush marks are running in the same direction down the wall. Each brush-load of paint will cover an area approximately 2 feet (60 cm) by 1 foot (30 cm) using this technique. Work across and then down the wall, painting adjacent areas and brushing them together.

If the brush feels dry, don't try to force paint out of it. Add more paint and blend it into the last wet area.

On most occasions, you will need two coats of paint to achieve a solid, flat finish.

Mottled coat of paint

FOR the impatient painter, there is an effective method of creating a paint effect with a soft mottled finish and only one coat of paint. This effect is subtle and can be used over a large wall area.

YOU WILL NEED

☐ Matte latex paint

☐ 4-inch (10-cm) paintbrush

1 Dip the paintbrush's bristles into the paint, scrape off one side of the brush on the side of the can, and brush dabs of paint onto the wall. Spread the dabs across an area approximately 2 feet (60 cm) square, transferring most of the paint on the brush onto the wall.

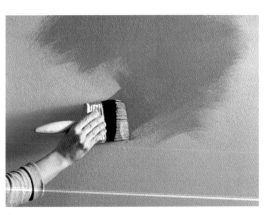

2 Twisting the angle of the paintbrush with every stroke, spread the dabs of paint out until they join up. The different angles of the brushstrokes and the varying intensity of the paint color will create the soft mottled effect desired.

Tinting paint

IF you want to paint stripes or even whole walls in graduated tones of a color, you are better off mixing your own colors. If you are mixing a pale color, always start with a white base, otherwise the colors may become too muddy. The technique is demonstrated here on small pots of paint, so that you can see exactly how much different quantities of colorizer affect the paint tones. Only small amounts of the colorizer are needed because it has a high pigment content.

The pigments in latex paints are quite crude and don't always mix together cleanly, but if you want to mix a darker color, they are the best starting point.

Buy paint in only the darkest tone of the colors you require, then add measured amounts of white paint to achieve the lighter shades. For a mid-tone, mix equal quantities of the color and white. For a light tone, add two parts white to one part color.

YOU WILL NEED

☐ White matte latex paint

☐ Paint pots or cans, one for each shade needed

☐ Tube of colorizer

☐ Small artist's paintbrush or a stirring stick for larger quantities of paint

1 Decant an equal amount of white paint into each pot or can. Even if you need less of one color, always mix equal amounts, or you will find it hard to judge the amount of colorizer needed to create each tone. Add a counted quantity of drops to the first can. Add double the number of drops to the next can, and continue, doubling the amount of colorizer added to each can until you have added colorizer to all of the paint cans.

2 Stir the paint and colorizer together until you get smooth, even colors. Always mix more than you will need, because it is almost impossible to exactly match the color again, and touch-ups may be required at a later date.

Masking

MASKING off is an important technique to master. It is used extensively throughout this book, and when done properly is an effective, and speedy, way of painting a straight line.

To mark a straight line on a wall, don't measure up at several points from the floor, or down from the ceiling, and then join the marked points. It is very unlikely that a line drawn in this way will be absolutely straight because the floors and ceilings are almost never completely true, especially in older homes. Also, this is a time-consuming procedure and discrepancies may creep in as you measure. Instead follow the directions on this page.

YOU WILL NEED

- ☐ Long spirit level with measurements marked along one edge
- ☐ Pencil
- ☐ Painting tape
- ☐ Matte latex paint
- ☐ 2-inch (5-cm) paintbrush

1 It is far more accurate, and easier and faster, to measure up, or down, at one point and then use a long spirit level to draw the line. Hold the level at the marked point, and adjust it until the bubble in the glass is perfectly central, then draw a pencil line along the level. Move the level along the wall, line one end up with the drawn line and adjust the other end until the bubble is central, then continue the pencil line. Repeat the process until you have completed the line needed.

2 Run a line of tape along the pencil line, on the opposite side to the one you want to paint. Position the tape a fraction of an inch below the line, so that when you paint the wall, the pencil mark will be covered. Smooth the tape down with your fingers so that is firmly stuck right along its length.

3 Dip the bristles of the paintbrush into the paint and wipe one side against the edge of the can. Never brush paint toward the tape. Either brush along it or brush from the tape in towards the center of the area. This avoids any paint being pushed under the edge of the tape and "bleeding" onto the background color.

Always remove the tape while the paint is still wet, carefully pulling it away to give a crisp, clean edge without tearing the surface of the dry paint underneath.

Storing paint

STORE excess paint for future touch-ups, especially if you have mixed a color. If there is a little paint left in a large can, decant it into a smaller jar or over time the paint will dry up. When there is a space between the level of paint in a vessel and the lid, cut a circle from a plastic bag and lay it on top of the wet paint. This will prevent air in the jar from drying out the top of the paint.

Collect jars, and ask friends to keep them for you, for storing your excess paint.

Cleaning tools and equipment

Clean brushes and rollers before using them for the first time and then as soon as you have finished a project. It takes a while for a brush or roller to "wear in" and stop shedding bristles, or pile. Therefore, the more the brush or roller is used, the better it becomes, as long as you clean it every time you use it. The cleaning procedure depends on the type of paint that you are using—oil-based is trickier to remove than water-based.

WATER-BASED PAINT

If you have to stop in the middle of a project, you can keep a roller covered in paint until you come back to it. The tray must be quite full of paint and the roller thoroughly coated in paint. Place the roller in the tray and put both into a large plastic bag. Press the bag down onto the surface of the paint, expelling any air. Tie the ends tightly and keep the tray flat.

On the other hand, a brush loaded with paint will start to harden within 10 minutes if left exposed to the air. A little more time can be bought if it's left standing in a paint can with the painted part of the bristles submerged, but this shouldn't be done for more than half an hour.

When you have finished the project, clean your brush and roller immediately.

YOU WILL NEED
- ☐ Household washing detergent
- ☐ Water

1 To clean a brush, rinse off excess paint under lukewarm, running water. Squeeze a little detergent onto the bristles and work it into a foam, rubbing the foam right into the bristles. Wash off the foam, parting the bristles to ensure that all the paint is washed away. Rinse until the water runs clean. Smooth the bristles into shape and leave to dry.

2 To clean a long-pile roller, rinse off the excess paint under lukewarm, running water. Squeeze a small amount of detergent onto the roller and work it into a foam, rubbing the foam well into the roller pile. Wash the foam off the roller, ensuring that every trace of paint is washed away. Rinse until the water runs clean. Leave to dry.

On a sponge roller, use the same procedure, rubbing the foam well into the sponge before rinsing it clean.

OIL-BASED PAINT

Brushes and rollers that you will use again with the same paint can be stored for several days in water. Put them into a bucket and ensure that the water completely covers them. This holds them in a state of suspended animation, but after a while the metal parts may rust. To use the brush or roller again, shake off the excess water, and then wipe or roll it onto newspaper until the water has been soaked up.

When it comes to final cleaning, oil-based paints on foam rollers makes them disposable, but brushes can be saved. Decant some paint thinner into a disposable container (an old paint can is ideal) and swish the brush around in this to rinse as much of the paint off as possible. Wash the brush, following the procedure for water-based paints, but using a lot of detergent. If the brush still feels sticky, repeat the whole process.

YOU WILL NEED
- ☐ Container
- ☐ Paint thinner
- ☐ Household washing detergent
- ☐ Water

ADDING TEXTURE

There are various texturizing mediums that can be applied to walls and ceilings to add decoration and cover damage. The different mediums can be applied in a variety of ways, but for the solutions given in this book there is only one technique to learn for each of the two types of texture used.

Textured wall covering

THIS is used to create a lightly textured top coat that will cover a damaged wall or ceiling. The trick lies in achieving the right amount of irregularity in the surface. Practice first on a board until you are comfortable with the technique, then move on to working on a wall or ceiling.

YOU WILL NEED

□ Textured wall covering
□ Paint can
□ 4-inch (10-cm) paintbrush
□ Grout float

1 Work in sections, approximately 1-foot (30-cm) square, across and then down the wall. Decant some textured wall covering into a paint can. Dip the 4-inch (10-cm) paintbrush into the covering, coating the bristles thickly. Dab the covering thickly onto the wall, across the section you are working on, transferring most of the covering on the brush onto the wall. Brush over the dabs, brushing the covering out into an even layer.

2 Hold the grout float at an angle so that only the long side edge comes into contact with the wall. Lightly smooth over the textured wall covering with long, sweeping strokes. If you have any excess on the float at the end of a stroke, wipe it off on the side of the paint can. Don't try to make the surface perfectly smooth; the irregularities are part of the effect.

When working into a corner or up to the baseboard or molding, apply the wall covering more thinly, and smooth it out a little more with the float, so that it's as thin as possible where it touches the corner or baseboard.

If the mixture moves around too easily, wait about 20 minutes for the surface to dry a little, then work over it again with the grout float. If the covering has dried too much in this time, spray the surface with water to make it mobile again.

Textured masonry paint

YOU WILL NEED

□ Textured masonry paint
□ Masonry roller
□ 3-inch (7.5-cm) paintbrush

To apply the textured paint evenly, it's best to use a masonry roller. The long hairs on these rollers give the paint a sponged effect, enhancing the sense of texture.

Roller the paint on using the *Rollering Paint* technique (see page 25). In inaccessible areas, brush on a thick coat of paint and stipple over it with the paintbrush to imitate the rollered texture.

WALLPAPERING

This can be quite a difficult procedure. If you want to paper a whole room with patterned wallpaper and have never done it before, it's better to hire a professional.

The technique illustrated here is for hanging plain lining paper, which has no pattern to worry about and is therefore easier to hang. If the walls are bare plaster, prime them beforehand using the *Mist Coat* technique (see page 25) to prevent the paste from being absorbed straight into the wall.

Hang a plumb line from the ceiling to establish a straight line. Measure the length of the wall and cut the drops of wallpaper at least 6 inches (15 cm) longer than the measured length to allow for trimming at the top and bottom.

1 Following the manufacturer's instructions, mix up the wallpaper paste and decant some into a tray. Use a sponge roller to apply the paste to one side of the lining paper, ensuring that it's evenly covered. Fold the top of the paper over and position it in the center of the length, sticking the pasted sides together. Repeat with the bottom half of the paper so that the ends meet in the middle. This will make handling and hanging easier. Following the wallpaper paste instructions, leave the paper to soak.

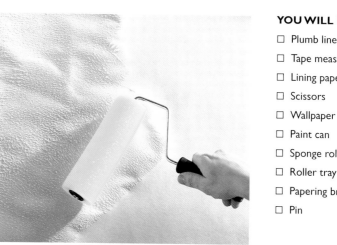

YOU WILL NEED

- ☐ Plumb line
- ☐ Tape measure
- ☐ Lining paper
- ☐ Scissors
- ☐ Wallpaper paste
- ☐ Paint can
- ☐ Sponge roller
- ☐ Roller tray
- ☐ Papering brush
- ☐ Pin

2 Carry the paper over to the wall, gently unstick one folded end and position it at the top of the wall, next to the plumb line. Ensure that the edge of the paper is parallel to the plumb line and brush the top section of the paper flat to the wall with the papering brush. Unstick the bottom section of the paper and brush this flat.

3 Always brush the paper from the middle out toward the edges, brushing out any air bubbles. If there is a bubble that won't brush out, don't force it. Pierce the paper in the center of the bubble with a pin, then gently brush the air toward the pin hole, and out of the bubble.

Where the paper overlaps the ceiling and baseboard, use the back of the scissors to mark the line. Pull the paper slightly away from the wall, cut off the excess with the scissors, and then smooth the paper back into place with the brush.

Repeat the process around the rest of the room, carefully lining up each new drop of paper with the edge of the last one.

TILING

On a wall, use a spirit level to establish a straight, horizontal line to start tiling from. If you are tiling above a work surface, check that it is level. If it is, use the work surface as the starting point. If it isn't level, draw a straight line just above it and tile up from that.

Fill any small gaps between the work surface and the bottom row of tiles with grout. Start tiling at the most visible end of the area you are working on, and if necessary, cut tiles to fit the space at the other end of the area.

YOU WILL NEED

- ☐ Spirit level
- ☐ Pencil
- ☐ Tile adhesive
- ☐ Adhesive spreader
- ☐ Tiles
- ☐ Tile spacers
- ☐ Tile cutter
- ☐ Ready-mixed grout
- ☐ Grout float
- ☐ Damp cloth
- ☐ Dry cloth

1 Working in an area approximately 1-foot (30-cm) square, scoop some tile adhesive out of the tub with the adhesive spreader and comb it out over the surface. Comb it into an even layer approximately ¼-inch (6-mm) thick.

2 Position the first tile at one end of the straight edge and press it down firmly. Place a tile spacer at the upper and lower corners of the tile, then place the next tile, butting it up to the spacers. Continue in this way until you have tiled the first row.

TILING TECHNIQUES

The same basic technique is used to tile all surfaces with all kinds of tiles, though some tiles require more care than others.

Terra-cotta tiles that are not sealed can be stained by grout, and similarly, heavily textured tiles can get grout trapped in the texture and require a lot of cleaning. So in both instances, apply the grout with the corner of the float between the tiles only.

The technique does vary a little if you are spacing tiles widely or using mosaic tiles, because you cannot use tile spacers. They are not big enough to give a wide gap between ordinary tiles, and produce a gap that is too wide between mosaic tiles. Instead follow the directions given here.

Decide on the gap you want between the tiles and cut a small piece of lumber to this size to use as a spacer. Spread a generous patch of adhesive on the surface where the first tile will be and press a tile into it. Use the spacer to establish the position of the next tile and repeat the process. Scoop up some grout with the float and press it down into the gaps between the tiles.

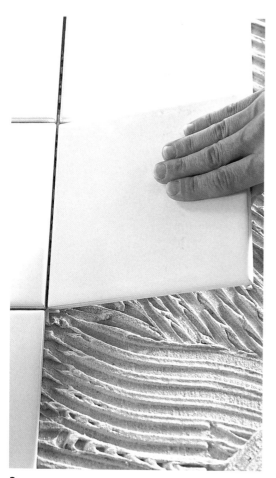

3 Use this row to position the next row, butting the tiles up to the spacers as before. When you have finished tiling, leave to dry.

4 Scoop some grout up onto the corner of the grout float. Spread it over the tiled surface, pressing it firmly down into the gaps between the tiles. Scrape one long side of the float over the surface to remove any excess grout, and leave it to harden.

5 When the grout is firm but not quite dry, wipe over the whole surface with a damp cloth, removing the bulk of any remaining excess from the front of the tiles. When completely dry, polish the whole surface with a dry cloth.

Left: *To space mosaic tiles, spread the adhesive over the area to be tiled, as above. Press the tiles down, leaving a gap of approximately $\frac{1}{8}$-inch (3-mm) between them. You will have to judge the gap by eye, but as it's so small, little discrepancies will not show.*

Right: *Scoop up just a little grout at a time on the float and grout the tiles as above.*

FLOORING

Laying some types of flooring, such as carpet, is a job best left to the professionals, but with care and time, you can try laying other types yourself. Remember that, unless the room is tiny, laying the floor will be a big task, so if you do decide to do the work yourself, allow plenty of time.

CARPET

It is always better to get a qualified fitter to lay carpet. The bulk and weight of a room-sized piece of carpet is huge, and if you cut it in the wrong place, there is nothing that you can do about it. In addition, stretching the carpet onto the gripper rods to make it smooth and straight isn't an easy task and you need special equipment.

WOODEN FLOORING

Laminate flooring usually comes in kit form, complete with all the instructions needed for that particular brand. Laminate isn't difficult to lay, though you do need to be able to cut straight lines with a saw. Read the instructions carefully and work methodically.

Real floorboards are a different matter. To lay these, it is usually best

Vinyl tiles

THESE are relatively easy to lay and to cut to fit at the edges of the room. Measure the space you need to fill and cut the tile to size with a sharp box cutter and a steel ruler.

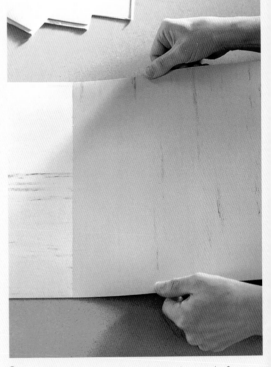

YOU WILL NEED

- ☐ Tape measure
- ☐ Pencil
- ☐ Self-adhesive vinyl tiles
- ☐ Steel ruler
- ☐ Box cutter

1 Peel the self-adhesive backing off each tile in turn. Lay the tile gently in position, and once you are sure that it's in the right place, press it down firmly with your hands. Butt the next tile right up to the first one and continue tiling, following the procedure explained above.

2 Vinyl tiles are available in various colors and often have surface markings in a contrast color. If you are using one main color, consider turning every second tile through 90 degrees, so that the markings on the tiles run at right angles to each other. This will make your floor a little more interesting.

to take up the old floorboards and lay the new ones on the existing joists. This is most definitely a job for a builder or carpenter, not one for a decorator.

TILES

Tiling a floor is quite a complicated process to get right, so spend time establishing the center of the floor and laying the first row of tiles.

Tiles are laid from the middle of the room outward. Draw a line across the room, from the measured center of one wall to the same point on the opposite wall. Draw another line at a right angle to the first between the center of the two remaining walls, forming a cross in the middle of the room.

Use this cross as a guide to position the first tile, fitting the corner of the tile into one quarter of the cross. Lay the next three tiles, fitting them into the remaining three quarters of the cross. Keeping the tiles on the line, lay more tiles along the first line, working from the middle four tiles out to the wall on either side of the cross. Use this first row to position the next row of tiles. Continue laying tiles in rows, working right up to the wall in one direction, then going back and working up to the wall in the other direction.

CERAMIC TILES

Unless you are working on the *Broken Tiles* solution (see page 75) or have previously tiled a floor, consider getting a professional in to lay ceramic tiles. Ceramic tiling a floor is more complicated, and expensive if you get it wrong, than tiling a wall and shouldn't be attempted by a novice.

Cork tiles

1 Working in sections approximately 2-feet (60-cm) square, scoop some adhesive up onto the spreader, and comb it out over the floor. Following the manufacturer's instructions, comb it into an even layer, approximately ⅛-inch (3-mm) thick.

2 Lay the first tile in position, and press it down with your hands. Butt the next tile up to it and continue tiling, following the procedure explained above.

CORK tiles are available only from specialty suppliers. Buy extras when you purchase them so you'll have some if you ever need replacements. Cork tiles are fairly easy to lay and fit. Cut them in the same way as vinyl tiles.

YOU WILL NEED
- ☐ Tape measure
- ☐ Pencil
- ☐ Cork tile adhesive
- ☐ Adhesive spreader
- ☐ Cork tiles
- ☐ Steel ruler
- ☐ Box cutter

WALLS COMPRISE the majority of the surface area of any room. They are usually the most dominant features in the room, too, being upright, at eye level, and the backdrop for all the furniture, fixtures, and many of the soft furnishings. The walls are also where most of us concentrate or originate our decorative schemes.

There are almost no limits to decorating wall surfaces, and when using the standard medium of paint, walls and the ceiling are the cheapest of all the household surfaces to cover. The problem most commonly associated with wall areas is surface damage; whether extensive or light, in a new or an old property, damage is a perennial problem.

The solutions to this problem tackle all levels of damage with practical, yet decorative finishes. There are solutions to suit both modern and traditional homes with all levels of damage. There are quick fix disguises and permanent cures, most of which can be tailored to suit any decorative scheme.

Another major wall problem centers on tiles, or the lack of them. In contrast to paint, these can be the most expensive way of covering a wall, and yet waterproofing in kitchens and bathrooms is usually essential. In this chapter you will find budget-conscious solutions, decorative disguises for unattractive tiles, and clever options for waterproofing with no tiles at all.

walls

THE PROBLEM: Uneven wall

This is a problem usually found in older properties, where the surface plaster has been affected by small, protracted movement and has become uneven over a long period of time, or where patch repairs have created uneven spots. As long as the plaster is just uneven, and not unsound, you don't have to go to the effort and expense of having the walls re-plastered. Paint effects, combining color and texture, come into their own in solving this problem. They can distract from the uneven appearance of the wall by encouraging the eye to linger on the decorative finish, rather than on the lumps and bumps.

SOLUTION 1: Two-color roller finish

THIS paint finish is simple and fast to apply, so it's suitable for even the most inexperienced painters. The mottled paint finish disguises any surface variations. The colors will mix as they are rolled on, so do a test on a board to check that the third shade (the one created by the two mixed colors), isn't too muddy.

YOU WILL NEED

☐ Roller tray

☐ Matte latex paint in two complementary colors (see page 23)

☐ Masonry roller

☐ 2-inch (5-cm) paintbrush

CORE TECHNIQUES

☐ Painting (see page 24)

Nature of problem:
uneven wall

Extent of solution:
visual disguise

Finish:
mottled colors

Time:
30 minutes

1 Pour 1 pint (600 ml) of each color of paint into opposite sides of the roller tray; they will sit next to each other without mixing too much. When you put the roller into the paint, always keep the handle pointing in the same direction, so that you don't blend the colors together in the tray.

2 Work across the wall in sections approximately 3-feet (1-m) square—though each section should be a roughly circular shape—to help avoid any hard lines. Roll the roller once through the tray, coating it thickly with the two paint colors. Then roll the paint onto the wall in single, long, spaced-apart strokes, transferring the majority of the paint onto the wall surface.

> **GETTING IT RIGHT**
>
> ● *Another color can be introduced by base-coating the wall in a third complementary color. Roller the two colors quite loosely over this base coat, keeping the effect dramatic and emphasizing the roller's texture.*
>
> ● *For corners and edges, where the roller doesn't quite fit, dip the end of the paintbrush into both paint colors in the tray, and then stipple them onto the wall, keeping the two-tone effect.*

3 Don't put the roller back into the paint. Instead, roll it lightly across the first strokes of paint on the wall, gently blending the colors together. Use the roller at different angles to create a subtle, dappled finish. The more you roll over the wet paint on the wall, the more the colors will blend and the subtler the effect will be.

The more contrast between the two colors you choose, the stronger the final visual effect will be. If the wall is generally, but gently, uneven, a subtle color contrast, like the one shown, will work well. If the wall is very uneven, choose strongly contrasting colors for a bold finish that will disguise bad patches more effectively.

SOLUTION 2: *Layered colorwash*

THE beauty of this paint effect is that it simply involves painting rather roughly, but in a certain order. The second coat covers any mistakes made in the first and refines the effect. Because the effect is built up from joined-up patches, the drier the surface is, the heavier the joins will be. However, the lighter these joins are, the better the finish, so you need to work quickly, and you shouldn't stop in the middle of a wall.

YOU WILL NEED

- ☐ White matte latex paint (see page 23)
- ☐ Long-pile roller
- ☐ Roller tray
- ☐ Paint can
- ☐ Wallpaper paste
- ☐ Matte latex paint in chosen color (see page 23)
- ☐ Stirring stick
- ☐ 4-inch (10-cm) paintbrush

CORE TECHNIQUES

- ☐ Painting (see page 24)

Nature of problem:
uneven wall

Extent of solution:
visual disguise

Finish:
mottled color

Time:
30 minutes

1 Using the long-pile roller, base coat the whole wall with white latex paint and leave it to dry. In the paint can, mix the wallpaper paste according to the manufacturer's instructions. Add the latex paint and stir thoroughly to create an even colorwash.

GETTING IT RIGHT

For a neat overall appearance, brush a little more paint along the edges against the ceiling, baseboard, and molding once the top coat is dry. This will make the edges look crisp and solid, and they will frame the paint effect cleanly.

2 Start working in a top corner. Dip about one-third of the paintbrush bristles into the colorwash, then scrape one side of them against the edge of the can to remove excess colorwash and avoid drips. Working in an area approximately 3-feet (1-m) square, dab the mixture on and immediately brush it out across the wall, alternating the angle of the paintbrush with each stroke to create a rough cloud shape. Move across the wall, repeating the process and brushing the cloud shapes together at their edges. Once you have painted right across the top section of the wall, move down, and then back across to cover the entire surface.

3 When the first layer of paint is completely dry, usually in about 4 hours, give the wall a second coat in the same way. To prevent the joins between the cloud shapes being very dark and prominent, ensure that the joins in the second coat don't lie directly over those in the first coat.

The base coat on the wall can be any color, but this color can greatly alter the look and tone of the finished paint effect. A white base coat won't alter the tones of your chosen color at all and is usually the best choice.

SOLUTION 3: *Painted rectangles*

THE combination of defined shapes and light texture in this dramatic wall treatment draw the eye away from the unevenness of the walls. The texture will also smooth over superficial damage, but if the wall has some cracks or pits, spot-fill them first (see page 51).

The rectangles work best on a fairly large scale, so make the largest ones proportional to the length of the wall, and the smallest ones about 3 feet (1 m) long by 10 inches (25 cm) wide. Spend some time planning the design of the rectangles on the wall before you start painting them.

Choose four colors: three shades of the same color and one contrasting color. The palest shade of the three will be the background color and the two darker shades, plus the contrasting color, will be used for the rectangles. The darkest and contrast color rectangles will overlap the lighter ones, giving depth to the treatment.

1 Using the long-pile roller, paint the entire wall in the background color. When the paint is dry, mark out a design of overlapping rectangles of different sizes. Use the spirit level and pencil to mark out the shapes — measurements are not necessary, only straight, level lines. If you are unhappy with any elements of the finished design, simply paint out the pencil lines and re-draw them.

3 Pour 1 pint (600 ml) of the mid-tone paint into the paint can and stir in a teaspoonful of fine, washed sand with the 1-inch (2.5-cm) paintbrush.

The contrasting color should always be of the same tonal value as the mid-tone of the three shades of the same color. This will prevent it from overpowering the overall effect and also stop it from being too insignificant.

2 Mask off the largest rectangles with painting tape. Mask off the entire rectangle; don't try to mask around any small rectangles that overlap it.

4 Using the 3-inch (7.5-cm) paintbrush, paint the masked-off rectangles. Brush the paint over the surface and then stipple it with the tips of the bristles to smooth out any brushstrokes and make the texture even. Remove the tape and leave the paint to dry.

For a coordinated decorative scheme, choose a contrast color that picks out an accent color used in any soft furnishings in the room.

YOU WILL NEED

- ☐ Matte latex paint in three shades of the same color (see page 23)
- ☐ Matte latex paint in a contrasting color (see page 23)
- ☐ Long-pile roller
- ☐ Roller tray
- ☐ Spirit level
- ☐ Pencil
- ☐ Painting tape
- ☐ Paint can
- ☐ Fine, washed sand
- ☐ 1-inch (2.5-cm) paintbrush
- ☐ 3-inch (7.5-cm) paintbrush

CORE TECHNIQUES

- ☐ Painting (see page 24)

Nature of problem: **uneven wall**

Extent of solution: **visual disguise**

Finish: **textured panels**

Time: **1½ hours**

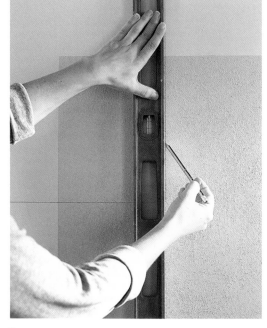

5 Again using the spirit level and pencil, re-draw the overlapping rectangles. Place the spirit level on the part of the line still visible on the background and draw along it, over the painted rectangle.

6 Mix 1 pint (600 ml) of the darkest shade of paint with fine sand, as before. Mask off, paint, and stipple the darkest rectangles. Finally, mask off and paint the contrast color rectangles in the same way.

SOLUTION 4: *Textured wallpaper*

BOLD texture in a defined shape will visually stand out from undulating, random texture and will distract from uneven walls. The strength of the effect depends on the size, shape, and colors used. Simple, geometric shapes are easy on the eye and easy to achieve, but if you want a more complex shape, make a template and use it to repeat the shape accurately.

YOU WILL NEED

☐ Textured wallpaper

☐ Tape measure

☐ Screw

☐ String

☐ Pencil

☐ Scissors

☐ Matte latex paint (see page 23)

☐ 2-inch (5-cm) paintbrush

☐ Wallpaper paste

☐ Sponge roller

☐ Roller tray

CORE TECHNIQUES

☐ Painting (see page 24)

☐ Wallpapering (see page 31)

Nature of problem:
uneven wall

Extent of solution:
visual disguise

Finish:
textured panels

Time:
2 hours

1 To cut a circle, measure from the middle of the wallpaper to one edge to determine the maximum radius. Tie one end of the piece of string to the screw and then tie the other end, at the measured length, to the pencil. Place the screw in the middle of the wallpaper and, keeping the string taut, rotate the pencil around the screw to draw a circle. The small hole will disappear when the wallpaper is painted.

3 Paint the circle with matte latex paint, applying two coats if necessary, and leave it to dry. Use the traditional wallpapering technique to paste the circles to the wall in your chosen arrangement.

GETTING IT RIGHT

When choosing the textured wallpaper, make sure that the pattern isn't larger than the shape that is going to be cut out of it, or the end result will look messy. It is best to choose a texture with no distinguishable pattern repeat. To keep the circles lined up, draw a vertical line on the wall along one side where they are to be placed, stick the first down, then measure the gap in between as you go along.

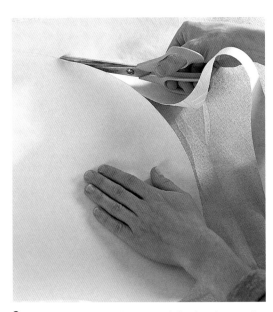

2 Cut out the circle with scissors, following the pencil line carefully so that the edge is smooth, and the circle is perfectly round.

For localized damage on a single wall, choose strong colors in a limited number of shapes to make a feature wall. If there is a lot of damage to cover on several walls, keep the background color and the color of the textured paper similar so as not to overpower the room. Painting the paper shapes before pasting them on will give a crisp finish and negate the need for careful painting or cutting in.

SOLUTION 5: *Fabric hanging*

A QUICK and very decorative solution for specific areas of unevenness is to cover the damaged section with a fabric hanging. This works best on a wall that doesn't have furniture against it. The secret of success with this solution lies in the choice of fabric. If the other soft furnishings in the room are in one color or a palette of subtle colors, a dramatic pattern can be used. On the other hand, if they are heavily patterned or in bright colors, choose a neutral color and texture, such as heavily woven wool. If you enjoy sewing, you could collect complementary, but different, remnants of fabric and make a patchwork hanging.

If appropriate, wash the fabric before making the hanging because it may not be pre-shrunk. If it isn't washable, you can have the hanging dry-cleaned from time to time.

For simplicity, make the width of the panel the width of the fabric, so that the selvedge edge saves sewing hems. Along the top and bottom edges, fold over and machine stitch a channel to accommodate your curtain rod at the top and a dowel at the bottom. If the fabric is very lightweight or the hanging very long, you may have to sew further channels at the halfway or one-third and two-third points and slide in more dowels to keep it hanging flat.

Dowels with decorative finials can be used to hang and weight the fabric; have the dowels cut wider than the hanging so that they protrude on one or both sides.

YOU WILL NEED

☐ Fabric the required size

☐ Sewing machine

☐ Sewing thread

☐ Curtain rod the width of the panel and brackets

☐ Dowel the width of the panel

Nature of problem:
uneven wall

Extent of solution:
physical disguise

Finish:
fabric panel

Time:
1 hour

THE PROBLEM: Damaged wall

This is a common problem in houses of all ages. The extent of the damage can range from old screw holes to extensive cracking. In newer properties plaster may not have been given time to dry before it was painted and so has cracked. In older properties plaster can simply decay, and if you try to remove old wallpaper, chunks of the plaster below can come away with it or become damaged as you scrape off the paper. There are several solutions to this problem, ranging from long-term fixes that take a little time but will cover heavier damage to quick and easy visual disguises. If, however, a wall is badly cracked, consult a builder because this may be a symptom of building problems that will need essential remedial work.

SOLUTION 1: *Heavy-grade lining paper*

HEAVY-GRADE lining paper is a good solution for a wall with extensive, yet shallow, damage. The marks made by a wallpaper scraper when removing old paper are typical of this kind of damage. They are enough to prevent you from simply painting the wall, but are extensive enough to make spot filling and sanding a chore. Lining paper will cover these marks and small pits, leaving a ready-to-paint surface. Use the traditional wallpapering technique to hang the paper.

YOU WILL NEED

- ☐ Heavy-grade lining paper (see page 23)
- ☐ Wallpaper paste
- ☐ Water
- ☐ Paint can
- ☐ Pasting brush
- ☐ Papering brush
- ☐ Seaming roller
- ☐ Sponge roller
- ☐ Roller tray
- ☐ Matte latex paint (see page 23)

CORE TECHNIQUES

- ☐ Wallpapering (see page 31)
- ☐ Painting (see page 24)

Nature of problem:
cracked or pitted wall

Extent of solution:
permanent cure

Finish:
smooth paper

Time:
3 hours

GETTING IT RIGHT

If you are concerned that the damage on your walls may show through the lining paper, you can cross-line for added coverage. This involves first hanging the paper in horizontal bands around the room, and then hanging a second layer vertically. The first layer can be difficult to get right and you should consider getting professional help.

Once hung, leave the lining paper to dry overnight before painting it to ensure that all of the paste has dried. Use the roller or brush to apply matte latex paint.

SOLUTION 2: *Picture collage bands*

THIS solution is ideal for small areas of light damage and is best used as a feature in an otherwise fairly plain room. Over a large area it becomes too overpowering. To avoid ruining original photographs, while still personalizing your collage, color photocopy some of your favorite pictures—photocopy paper is also thin and easier to paste than photographs.

Choose a base color in a strong tone and paint the wall with two coats. Using a pencil and ruler, mark the edges of the bands of collage on the wall. Brush a thin coat of border adhesive onto the back of each photocopy. Then position each one on the wall, slightly overlapping them and covering the pencil lines. Finally, varnish the photocopies to prevent the colors from fading over time.

GETTING IT RIGHT

To create a torn edge, take the photocopy in both hands and, keeping the left hand still, pull the right hand toward you. Keep your hands close together to control the tearing.

For the most effective collage choose images with a color or visual theme, rather than just a random selection.

YOU WILL NEED

- ☐ Matte latex paint (see page 23)
- ☐ Long-pile roller
- ☐ Roller tray
- ☐ Color photocopies
- ☐ Ruler
- ☐ Pencil
- ☐ Border adhesive
- ☐ 1-inch (2.5-cm) paintbrush
- ☐ Papering brush
- ☐ Water-based varnish

CORE TECHNIQUES

- ☐ Wallpapering (see page 31)

Nature of problem:
cracked or pitted wall

Extent of solution:
permanent cure

Finish:
colorful bands

Time:
2 hours

SOLUTION 3: *Rough plaster effect*

1 Mix your own textured paint by stirring joint compound into latex paint. Pour 1 pint (600 ml) of paint into the can and add the compound a little at a time, stirring it in with the 1-inch (2.5-cm) paintbrush. Make sure that the mixture is well mixed, with no lumps. Add more compound until the paint is a stiff yet movable consistency. Don't mix more than 1 pint (600 ml) at a time, or it might harden before you can use it.

GETTING IT RIGHT

- *Keep the brushstrokes similar lengths, twisting your hand at the wrist for consistent and easy application with alternating angles.*
- *On heavily damaged sections of wall you may need to apply a thicker layer of textured paint. To do this, hold the brush almost parallel to the wall and lay the mixture onto the surface.*

2 Using the 4-inch (10-cm) paintbrush, apply the textured paint to the wall. Dip the bristles into the paint and scrape off the excess on one side. Start at the top of the wall and work across and then down it, brushing on the paint with short strokes. Make sure that all the brushstrokes are at alternating angles to keep the effect looking unstructured. You only need to apply one coat, but if the paint doesn't fill a crack when you first brush it on, add more mixture and work over the brushstroke again until it looks right.

YOU can turn the tables and take advantage of heavy surface damage to walls: use textured paint to fill and smooth the worst pits and cracks and create an overall rough plaster effect. This is a one-coat solution, incorporating cover and color together, so there is no need to paint the wall later.

While this is the quickest solution for covering really bad walls, if at any stage in the future you want to change the surface, re-plastering is the only option.

If some of the cracks still show through when the paint is dry or the texture appears too light in places, simply mix up some more paint and joint compound and work over these areas again, feathering the paint at the edges.

YOU WILL NEED

- ☐ Paint can
- ☐ Matte latex paint (see page 23)
- ☐ Joint compound
- ☐ 1-inch (2.5-cm) paintbrush
- ☐ 4-inch (10-cm) paintbrush

CORE TECHNIQUES

- ☐ Painting (see page 24)

Nature of problem:
cracked or pitted wall

Extent of solution:
permanent cure

Finish:
heavy texture

Time:
1 ½ hours

SOLUTION 4: *Lightly textured top coat*

THIS is a good solution for badly damaged walls because you can cover absolutely all damage by skimming a top layer over the surface. This technique is also easy to apply to large areas. The aim is to produce a consistent, undulating finish across the whole wall that will look intentional, and not accidental. The light texture will fit well into a traditional or modern interior and is a suitable surface for flat color or a paint effect.

1 Work in easy-to-manage sections, approximately 1 foot (30 cm) square, across the wall. Using the paintbrush, apply the textured wall covering thickly onto the wall, then brush it out to form an even layer.

2 Hold the grout float at an angle, so that only the long side edge is in contact with the wall. Lightly smooth over the textured wall covering with long, sweeping strokes. Don't try to make the surface perfectly smooth; the irregularities are part of the effect.

YOU WILL NEED

- ☐ Textured wall covering (see page 23)
- ☐ 4-inch (10-cm) paintbrush
- ☐ Grout float
- ☐ Matte latex paint (see page 23)
- ☐ Long-pile roller
- ☐ Roller tray

CORE TECHNIQUES

- ☐ Adding texture (see page 30)
- ☐ Painting (see page 24)

Nature of problem:
cracked or pitted wall

Extent of solution:
permanent cure

Finish:
light texture

Time:
2 ½ hours

Leave the wall to dry overnight and then, using the long-pile roller, paint it with latex paint. Because the surface is highly absorbent, it needs the paint to seal it. Therefore, always apply two coats of paint, even if the color looks solid after one coat.

GETTING IT RIGHT

- When working into a corner or down to the baseboard, feather out the wall covering so that it is as thin as possible where it touches the corner or baseboard.
- If the mixture moves too easily and it's difficult to create a flattened finish, wait about 20 minutes for the surface to dry a little, then work over it again. If you find that the surface has dried too much, spray it with water.

SOLUTION 5: *Spot filling and sanding*

I Smooth spackle over the damaged area, making sure that it covers all the holes and cracks. Use the trowel to smooth the spackle as much as possible, but it is better for it to be slightly raised at this stage, because it may sink back slightly when it dries. Leave it to dry; the time depends on the thickness of the spackle and the room temperature.

WHEN the damage to a wall is localized and specific, spot filling then sanding will restore an overall smoothness. This kind of damage is common after re-wiring or removing picture hooks or screws. The vital part of this solution to get right is applying the spackle. If you apply too much, it will form a raised spot and will need extensive sanding, making a smooth finish more difficult to achieve. Too little and it will dry shallow of the surface and a second application will be necessary. The ideal is for the filler to dry very slightly raised, so that it both fills the hole and needs little sanding.

Unless you are very good at this technique, it's unlikely that you will be able to make the filled patch perfectly flat to the original wall, but take time to fill and sand carefully and the bumps will be barely noticeable.

2 Sand the spackle smooth, paying particular attention to the area where it meets the original surface. Paint the entire wall.

GETTING IT RIGHT

Details, such as replacing standard light switches with stylish ones, will make an enormous difference to a decorating scheme. Remember that a qualified electrician should do all electrical work.

To check the smoothness of the finish, run your hand over the area; your fingers will detect bumps better than your eyes. If, once painted, depressions become more obvious, fill and paint them again.

YOU WILL NEED

☐ Spackle
☐ Small trowel
☐ 120-grit sandpaper
☐ Matte latex paint (see page 23)
☐ Long-pile roller
☐ Roller tray

CORE TECHNIQUES

☐ Painting (see page 24)

Nature of problem:
cracked or pitted wall

Extent of solution:
permanent cure

Finish:
smooth wall

Time:
30 minutes

SOLUTION 6: *Faux paneling*

Tʜɪs is an ideal solution for an older or more traditionally styled house. It is a little more time-consuming to undertake, but will add real elegance and an increased sense of perspective to the space. Because the MDF (medium density fiberboard) is so smooth, any light damage that will be visible between the panels should be repaired by spot filling. To measure, draw a border 4 inches (10 cm) in from the molding, baseboard, and dado rail. Take the length and divide it up into equal panels approximately 12 inches (30 cm) wide, with 3-inch (7.5-cm) spaces between them. There is a little leeway here; the spacing can vary several inches (cm) either way without affecting the final look. If necessary, you can add a half panel at one end to fill the area neatly.

1 Ask your lumberyard to cut the MDF to size for you. The majority of yards offer this service, and their machine-cut edges will make your panels look much more professional.

If you have to deal with an area around stairs, first have the panels cut to the full length. Then, following the line of the dado at the top and the baseboard at the bottom, use the adjustable T-square to measure the angle of the stairs and transfer these angles onto the board. The marked-up board will be a parallelogram. Cut along the marked lines with the jigsaw and sand the edges smooth.

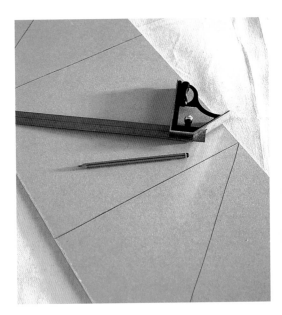

YOU WILL NEED

- ☐ ¼-inch (6-mm) thick MDF
- ☐ Pencil
- ☐ Tape measure
- ☐ Adjustable T-square
- ☐ Jigsaw
- ☐ 120-grit sandpaper
- ☐ Project glue
- ☐ Spackle
- ☐ Matte latex paint (see page 23)
- ☐ Paintbrush

Nature of problem:
cracked or pitted wall

Extent of solution:
permanent cure

Finish:
raised panels

Time:
3 ½ hours

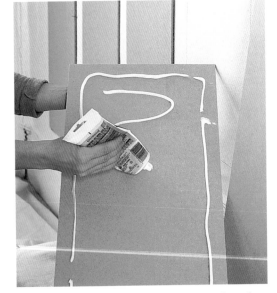

2 Working on one panel at a time, squeeze a line of project glue around the edges, and a further swirl down the middle.

3 Following your pencil marks, position the panel on the wall. Press it firmly in place to ensure that the glue is in full contact with the wall.

Paneling is traditionally only placed below the dado rail, but the upper part of a wall can be paneled using the same method for a more formal look.

4 If a panel won't sit flat on an uneven section of wall, hammer in small nails at an angle across the edge to hold it in place while the glue dries.

5 Spread a line of spackle around the edge of each panel, covering the line between the panel and the wall and filling any larger gaps where the wall is uneven. Smooth the spackle and leave to dry. Paint the entire wall, including the panels, the same color.

SOLUTION 7: *Canvas panel*

COVER damage and add style with a large canvas. It is a good solution for heavy but localized damage, where a window has been blocked up, for example. Measure the damaged area and make the canvas large enough to cover it. An easy design is simple, graphic, and in colors compatible with the room.

YOU WILL NEED

- ☐ 2 lengths of 1 x 2 (2.5 x 5 cm) boards the length of the panel
- ☐ 2 lengths of 1 x 2 (2.5 x 5 cm) boards the width of the panel minus 2 inches (5 cm)
- ☐ 4 corner plates
- ☐ Bradawl
- ☐ 16 ¾-inch (2-cm) screws
- ☐ Piece of canvas the length and width of the panel plus 4 inches (10 cm) each side
- ☐ Staple gun
- ☐ Matte latex paints
- ☐ 1-inch (2.5-cm) paintbrush
- ☐ String, pencil, and compass

Nature of problem:
cracked or pitted wall

Extent of solution:
physical disguise

Finish:
painted panel

Time:
4 hours

1 Narrow side up, lay the short lengths of lumber between the ends of the long lengths. Lay a corner bracket over each butted corner and use the bradawl to mark the position of the holes. Drive a screw through each hole.

3 Fold the corners as shown to give a neat finish. Staple the corner canvas to the frame. After applying two basecoats, paint the canvas with your chosen design.

2 Lay the canvas out flat and place the lumber frame in the middle of it. On one side, fold the canvas over to the back of the frame and, in the middle of that side, fire a staple through it into the narrow side of the lumber. Stretch the canvas taut and repeat the process on the opposite side of the frame. Do the same on the remaining two sides. Go back to the first side and, working out in one direction and then the other from the center staple, staple the canvas to the frame, stopping 2 inches (5 cm) from the corners. Repeat on the opposite side and then on the other two sides of the frame.

GETTING IT RIGHT

- ● *On larger frames, you will need cross braces so that the frame doesn't bow under the strain of the stretched canvas. These should be attached, flat side up at the back, by nailing through the outside of the main frame into the end of the strut, at both ends. A canvas that measures 2 x 2 feet (60 x 60 cm) needs no struts. A canvas that measures 2 x 4 feet (60 cm x 1.2 m) needs one strut bracing the length. One measuring 4 x 4 feet (1.2 x1.2 m) needs two struts in a cross shape.*

- ● *If canvas isn't available, heavy-weight cotton is perfectly suitable and only a little more expensive.*

For a simple design, use the string and pencil method (see page 44) to mark out large quarter and half circles and draw around dinner plates to mark out small half circles. Paint the shapes with latex paints in colors to complement your decorative scheme.

THE PROBLEM: **Plain tiles**

Tiles are available in a wealth of sizes, styles, and prices, and depending on the finish you want, tiling a large area can be expensive. The cheapest and most commonly used tiles are plain, white, 6-inch (15-cm) square tiles. These will produce a perfectly sound surface, but not a very interesting one. However, if budget dictates that these are the tiles to use, there are two solutions to choose from, both of which will make the most of the plainest tiles. If the area to be tiled is uneven, affecting the finish, the tiles can be applied to a board cut to the exact size required, which can then be fixed to the wall using strong project glue.

SOLUTION 1: *Plain tiles and colored grout*

Aᴅᴅ color and style to plain tiles by spacing them widely for a more rustic, less institutional feel and by using colored grout. Of course, this will also use far fewer tiles, so you may be able to buy nicer tiles on the same budget.

1 Once you have tiled the area and the adhesive has dried, mix up the grout. Add the powder grout to the water, following the manufacturer's instructions. Never add water to powder, because that makes it difficult to mix in all the lumps of powder.

2 Stir the mixture thoroughly until all the lumps have disappeared and the mixture is smooth.

YOU WILL NEED

- ☐ Tile adhesive
- ☐ Adhesive spreader
- ☐ Tiles (see page 23)
- ☐ Wide-gap powder grout
- ☐ Water
- ☐ Stirring stick
- ☐ Grout float
- ☐ Damp cloth
- ☐ Dry cloth

CORE TECHNIQUES

- ☐ Tiling (see page 32)

Nature of problem:
plain tiles

Extent of solution:
physical enhancement

Finish:
smooth tiles

Time:
2 hours

3 Scoop up some grout on the end of the grout float and smooth it over the tiles, spreading generous amounts into the gaps between them. Use the edge of the float to lift excess grout off the tiles, leaving the whole surface as smooth as possible. Because the gaps are wide, achieving a flat finish can be difficult. To overcome this, leave the grout slightly high and let it harden a little—for no more than 1 hour—and then wipe over it gently with a damp cloth, rubbing until it is smooth.

4 Leave to dry until the surface of the grout has hardened enough to wipe the excess off the tiles with a damp cloth without affecting the surface of the grout. Leave to dry completely, and then polish off any grout residue with a dry cloth.

GETTING IT RIGHT

Because the gaps between tiles are so wide, you must use a special wide-gap grout, usually available only in powder form. This style of tiling is best used in areas that do not get too wet—above a work surface rather than behind a sink, for example—as dirty water and oils will mark the grout. Because there is so much visible grout in this solution, marks can be a problem.

Grout will account for a great deal more of the surface area than usual, so bear in mind the color balance between it and the tile color: if the grout color is too strong, the end result will be an overbearing grid effect.

SOLUTION 2: *Mosaic border*

Mosaic tiles will add interest to plain tiles and used sparingly, are a budget-conscious solution. Do consider the overall effect. Too many colors will overwhelm the plain tiles, as will too strong a color or too many rows of mosaic, so experiment with positioning the tiles before sticking them.

Add the mosaic border above the top row of plain tiles, although the profiles will not be flush because mosaic tiles are thinner than standard tiles.

1 Spread tile adhesive over the area where the mosaic tiles will lie, working in small areas at a time so that it doesn't start to dry before you get to it. Starting from one end, press the mosaic tiles into the adhesive. Keep the spacing quite tight and judge the gaps by eye. Leave to dry.

If you have tiled onto a board that has then been fastened to the wall, finish the top edge neatly with a row of horizontal tiles fastened in place in the same way as the border.

2 Scoop some grout up with one corner of the grout float and smooth it out over the tiles, pressing it down into the small gaps between the tiles until they are completely filled. When the grout is firm but not completely dry, wipe away the excess with the damp cloth. Leave to dry and then polish off any grout residue with a dry cloth.

GETTING IT RIGHT

If the adhesive protrudes up between the mosaic tiles, leave it to dry for approximately 10 minutes and then brush away any excess with a soft brush, being careful not to move the tiles in the process.

YOU WILL NEED

☐ Tile adhesive
☐ Adhesive spreader
☐ Mosaic tiles (see page 23)
☐ Ready-mixed grout
☐ Grout float
☐ Damp cloth
☐ Dry cloth

CORE TECHNIQUES

☐ Tiling (see page 32)

Nature of problem:
plain tiles

Extent of solution:
physical enhancement

Finish:
mosaic band

Time:
1 hour

THE PROBLEM: Unattractive tiles

When buying a property, you are quite likely to inherit some tiled surfaces with it. If you are lucky, these are attractive or at worst, plain. However, you may well face the problem of tiles in out-dated colors and patterns, or even with textured finishes. There are two different solutions for these problems, both of which avoid the expense and aggravation of removing the old tiles and replacing them with new ones.

Both solutions are also fairly quick, so even if you do intend to replace the tiles at some point in the future when the budget allows, it may be worth treating them in the interim.

SOLUTION 1: *Painted a solid color*

1 Working in sections about 3-feet (1-m) square and using the paintbrush, paint primer around the edges of each tile, totally covering the grout.

If you are painting the tiles a color other than white, the primer can be tinted to go with that color. Immediately roller a little more primer over the tiles, obliterating the brushstrokes to create a smooth surface. Leave to dry.

2 Paint and then roller over the tiles with satin paint in the same way. The roller applies in a thin layer, so if the tiles were a dark or strong color, more coats will be needed.

If the primer is tinted, don't get the topcoat on the recessed grout lines.

Leave to dry and then roller over the whole surface with high-gloss clear enamel, again avoiding the grout lines. Leaving the primer in the grout lines with a matte finish will imitate the matte finish of real grout against the high-gloss finish of ceramic tiles.

If inherited tiles are smooth, sound, and well laid, but an unattractive color, you can simply paint them. To keep the surface looking smooth, use a gloss roller to apply the primer, satin paint, and gloss enamel.

You can use a color other than white, but remember that pastels generally don't look good, so choose rich or deep tones.

YOU WILL NEED

☐ Primer
☐ 1-inch (2.5-cm) paintbrush
☐ Gloss roller
☐ Satin paint
☐ High-gloss clear enamel

CORE TECHNIQUES

☐ Painting (see page 24)

Nature of problem:	**unattractive tiles**
Extent of solution:	**physical disguise**
Finish:	**flat color**
Time:	**2 hours**

GETTING IT RIGHT

If you want to use a color other than white, look at displays of tiles in tile shops and match the paint color to a real tile color in a display that you like.

The best color choice for painted tiles is white, as this works on both the tiles and the grout, and it also gives the cleanest overall appearance.

SOLUTION 2: *Colored with gilt cream*

THE most unfortunate tiles to inherit are those with a textured finish, because flat color will emphasize the pattern. However, using bold metallic tones modernizes the tiles and distracts from the pattern. The pattern is secondary, overwhelmed by the silver color and softened by the mottled finish. The consistency of gilt cream is the same as shoe polish, and you apply it in exactly the same way.

YOU WILL NEED

☐ Dark-gray primer
  (or black colorizer
  and white primer if
  the required primer
  color is unavailable)

☐ 1-inch (2.5-cm)
  paintbrush

☐ Soft cloth

☐ Silver and pewter
  gilt creams

☐ High-gloss clear
  enamel

☐ Gloss roller

☐ Roller tray

CORE TECHNIQUES

☐ Painting (see page 24)

Nature of problem:
unattractive tiles

Extent of solution:
visual disguise

Finish:
mottled metallic color

Time:
2 hours

1 Use dark-gray primer under the gilt cream. This is commercially available, but if your local store doesn't stock it, it's easy to mix your own by tinting white primer with the black colorizer. These are strong color pigments, so add a little at a time and stir it in until you reach the right shade.

2 Using the paintbrush, paint the tiles with tinted primer, ensuring that you completely cover the grout between the tiles. If the color of the original tiles is very strong, the primer may look patchy, so apply a second coat. Leave it to dry.

3 Fold the cloth over your index finger and dip it into the gilt cream. Dab cream onto a tile and rub it over the surface using a circular motion and totally covering the tile. Rub along the edges of the tiles, keeping the cloth flat over your finger to avoid pushing cream down into the recessed grout lines.

Rub pewter gilt cream over the silver cream in the same way, but only in small patches so that it doesn't totally cover the silver and gives a mottled effect. Leave it to harden overnight.

Using the gloss roller, apply a coat of high-gloss clear enamel over the tiles, again ensuring that the grout lines aren't covered.

GETTING IT RIGHT

If the grout between some of the tiles is raised and you rub some gilt cream or roller some gloss onto it by accident, complete the painting process then paint the grout a dark gray matte color with a fine brush and the tinted primer.

This quick, simple solution has turned bright orange tiles into modern metallic ones, perfect for a contemporary kitchen.

THE PROBLEM: Low-budget tiling

The quality and prices of tiles vary greatly, and your preferred scheme may be considerably compromised by your budget. Tackle this problem by making cheaper tiles more decorative in themselves. Change the shape, use a range of colors, or add different-sized tiles in patterns or bands. This approach not only provides a more visually appealing look, but also distracts from the poorer quality of the cheaper tiles.

SOLUTION 1: *Mosaic bands*

THIS solution uses bands of mosaic to pad out the main tiles, so you need fewer of them. Tile the area as described for *Plain Tiles and Colored Grout* (see page 56), with gaps of 1½ inches (4 cm) between the main tiles. Then use the narrow edge of the adhesive spreader to spread more adhesive between the main tiles and position the mosaic tiles, spacing them evenly between the edges of the main tiles. When the adhesive is dry, grout all the tiles.

Mosaic tiles are available in a wide range of colors, so it's usually easy to choose some to complement the color of the main tiles. For a softer, more rustic appearance the mosaic tiles can be used upside down, leaving the grooved backs visible.

YOU WILL NEED

- ☐ Tiles (see page 23)
- ☐ Mosaic tiles (see page 23)
- ☐ Tile adhesive
- ☐ Adhesive spreader
- ☐ Ready-mixed grout
- ☐ Grout float
- ☐ Damp sponge
- ☐ Dry cloth

CORE TECHNIQUES

- ☐ Tiling (see page 32)

Nature of problem:
low budget

Extent of solution:
permanent cure

Finish:
different-sized tiles

Time:
3 hours

SOLUTION 2: *Broken-tile tiling*

1 Break up the tiles by hitting them sharply in the center with the hammer. Wear safety goggles when doing this, because pieces of tile can fly up. Break up all the tiles and put the different colors into piles so that it's easy to find the color and shape you want later. You may prefer to wear gloves when handling the broken tiles, because the edges can be sharp.

2 Spread the tile adhesive over the area to be tiled. Start tiling at the corners, pressing the pieces of tile into the adhesive. Work around the sides and then in toward the middle, choosing different colored pieces from the piles and building up a pattern. Leave to dry.

> **GETTING IT RIGHT**
>
> *Use pieces of tile with the original smooth corner to establish the corners of the tiled area. Use pieces with an original smooth edge along the sides. This ensures that the perimeter of the tiled area has no sharp edges.*

3 Squeeze the grout straight from the tube into the gaps between the tiles. Using the grout float, smooth the grout down to fill the gaps completely. When it's dry, wipe away the excess with the damp sponge and then polish the surface with the dry cloth.

So as not to overwhelm the tiles, make sure that the grout color isn't the darkest of all the shades used.

GROUPING complementary shades together in random shapes will enhance cheaper tiles, and colored grout will detract from the poorer finish. In addition, broken tiles are filled out with more grout lines, so you need fewer to tile an area than you would if you used them conventionally. The key to this solution is planning, so play with the positioning until the shapes fit neatly together, and the colors are balanced.

YOU WILL NEED

- ☐ Tiles
- ☐ Hammer
- ☐ Safety goggles
- ☐ Protective gloves
- ☐ Tile adhesive
- ☐ Adhesive spreader
- ☐ Ready-mixed colored grout
- ☐ Grout float
- ☐ Damp sponge
- ☐ Dry cloth

CORE TECHNIQUES

- ☐ Tiling (see page 32)

Nature of problem:
low budget

Extent of solution:
permanent cure

Finish:
colorful tiles

Time:
6 hours

THE PROBLEM: **Waterproofing**

If you need to waterproof a small area, a back splash behind a sink for example, but tiling it is just too expensive or the wall surface is not sound enough to allow it, there are alternative solutions, all characterized by their simplicity. Each solution can be achieved with the minimum of fuss and at little expense, while at the same time adding an extra dimension to the room's decorative scheme.

The painted solutions have immense flexibility and can be customized and colored to fit any area. The hard surface solutions should be professionally cut to the desired shape and dimensions.

SOLUTION 1: *Gloss-varnished panel*

Tʜɪs is the cheapest of the solutions. The enamel dries to a hard, waterproof, glossy finish and is incredibly versatile because it is applied in the same way as paint. Mask off a shape or paint the area freehand to create curves or specific patterns.

Paint the entire wall with matte latex paint and leave to dry. Measure and mark out the area to be waterproofed and mask it off with painting tape. Brush high-gloss clear enamel over the masked area. Remove the tape immediately and leave to dry. Repeat the process with a second coat of enamel.

If any enamel bleeds under the tape, leave it to dry and paint over it with latex paint.

The enamel will deepen any color it's painted over quite considerably, so you may want to test the effect on a board before painting the whole wall.

YOU WILL NEED

☐ Matte latex paint (see page 23)

☐ Long-pile roller

☐ Roller tray

☐ Painting tape

☐ 1-inch (2.5-cm) paintbrush

☐ High-gloss clear enamel

CORE TECHNIQUES

☐ Painting (see page 24)

Nature of problem:
no tiles

Extent of solution:
permanent cure

Finish:
glossy panel

Time:
30 minutes

SOLUTION 2: *Shaped plastic back splash*

Gᴇᴛ the plastic professionally cut—most suppliers will be able to do this for you. Experiment with different shapes on paper until you are happy with one and give that to the supplier as a template. Mark the points where you want holes drilled for the fixings and use wall plugs and mirror screws to attach it to the wall.

> **GETTING IT RIGHT**
>
> *A line of clear sealant should be applied to the join between the plastic and the top of the sink, to ensure that no damp gets behind the back splash.*

This shape is made by drawing a circle with a diameter of the widest part of the sink. This is bisected below the center, at the point where it's the exact width of the back of the sink. Use chrome-headed mirror screws to fasten it to the wall.

YOU WILL NEED

☐ ¼-inch (6-mm) plastic cut to shape and drilled

☐ Chrome mirror (or mounting) screws

☐ Wall plugs

☐ Drill

☐ Drill bit

Nature of problem:
no tiles

Extent of solution:
permanent cure

Finish:
transparent back splash

Time:
10 minutes

SOLUTION 3: *Metal back splash*

Tʜᴇ perfect solution for a sleek, modern room, this is especially suitable in kitchens where hard-looking materials are more appropriate. Simply measure the area and ask the metal supplier to cut a piece of brushed steel to the right size. Fix this to the wall with epoxy adhesive.

YOU WILL NEED

☐ Metal panel cut to size

☐ Epoxy adhesive

Nature of problem:
no tiles

Extent of solution:
permanent cure

Finish:
metal back splash

Time:
20 minutes

The metal surface will also reflect light in the often dark area behind a sink under wall units.

SOLUTION 3: *Faux-tiled back splash*

THIS is a good solution if you are on a tight budget. Work on a board that can be fastened to the wall. The effect of handmade tiles can be created with thick paint. High-gloss enamel will toughen the surface and imitate the glossy finish of glazed tiles. The background "grout" color should be left in eggshell.

YOU WILL NEED

- ☐ Particle board
- ☐ 120-grit sandpaper
- ☐ Sanding block
- ☐ 1-inch (2.5-cm) paintbrush
- ☐ Large stippling brush
- ☐ 1-inch (2.5-cm) square-ended, flat paintbrush
- ☐ Eggshell paint in two tones of dark gray and in white
- ☐ One-coat satin paint in two colors
- ☐ Ceramic wall tile
- ☐ Pencil
- ☐ Plastic teaspoon
- ☐ Small stippling brush
- ☐ High-gloss clear enamel
- ☐ Project glue

Nature of problem:
no tiles

Extent of solution:
permanent cure

Finish:
tile effect

Time:
3 hours

1 Measure the area to be tiled and divide this by 4 inches (10 cm) to work out the number of "tiles" you will paint. The remaining space can be divided up to make the grout lines; ideally these should be about ¼-inch (6-mm) wide. Cut the board to size and sand the sharp edges and corners.

2 Using the 1-inch (2.5-cm) paintbrush, undercoat the board with the darkest gray eggshell paint. Then stipple the surface with the lighter gray eggshell paint. Use the large stippling brush in short, dabbing strokes to create a mottled finish.

3 Place the ceramic tile in one corner of the board and draw around it. Leaving a ¼-inch (6-mm) gap (or whatever you have calculated in Step 1) to simulate the grout line, re-position the tile next to the drawn shape and draw around it again. Continue moving and drawing around the tile across the board, leaving the same size gap each time. Leaving a horizontal grout line, repeat the process on the next row up, and until the whole board is covered with drawn tiles.

4 Working on one drawn tile at a time, spoon paint into the center of the tile: you will need approximately 1 heaped teaspoon of paint per tile. For this board, the tiles were painted in alternate colors.

5 Use the 1-inch (2.5-cm) flat, square-ended artist's paintbrush to push the paint out to the edges of the drawn tile. Push the paint right up to the pencil line, but don't try to brush it out smoothly. Repeat the process on all of the alternate squares.

6 Using the other paint color, spoon and then push paint to the edges of the remaining drawn tiles, creating a checkerboard effect. Leave to dry for 48 hours.

7 Mix a little white paint into each color to make slightly lighter tones. Dip the tips of the small stippling brush into the appropriate mix, wipe the brush on a cloth until it's almost dry, then lightly rub over random patches of the tile.

This solution can be worked straight onto a wall, but the tile colors must be built up in thin layers to prevent them running down the surface.

8 Using the 1-inch (2.5-cm) flat, square-ended artist's paintbrush, apply the enamel to the painted tiles, taking care not to get varnish on the grout lines.

THE SECONDARY AREA of visual importance in any room is the floor because, along with the walls, it makes up the main focus of most rooms. It forms a continuous surface throughout the house and is usually sectioned up room by room. The floor is also the surface that receives the most wear and tear. Some rooms may require or benefit from a hard flooring surface, while others can accommodate a softer covering.

Unfortunately, choosing a floor covering of any type invariably involves considerable expense. Whenever possible, it's wise to find permanent solutions that make the most of your existing flooring at a fraction of the cost of covering or replacing it.

This chapter looks at concrete floors, carpets, and traditional floorboards and offers a range of solutions to the problems of damage and dirt while bearing budget firmly in mind. Some solutions involve paint effects; although these look sophisticated, they are very easy to achieve and actually work best if painted quite roughly.

Baseboards, hiding at the foot of most of our walls, have problems of their own and there are ingenious solutions for tackling them, too.

floors

THE PROBLEM: Concrete floor and a low budget

Many modern homes have poured concrete floors, particularly in basements and sunrooms. Concrete is a cold and unattractive material that really needs to be covered or at the very least disguised. The obvious choice is laying a wooden floor, ceramic floor tiles, or carpet—all of which can be expensive. However, there are some inexpensive and creative solutions to this problem that offer an appealing decorative element to rooms that need practical, water-resistant flooring or have heavy traffic.

SOLUTION 1: *Checkered cork tiles*

CORK tiles offer a warm and cost-effective covering for a concrete floor. Buy tiles that haven't been sealed and paint over them, ensuring that the paint fills all the interstices. You will need two coats for a solid finish. Let the paint dry overnight and then lay the floor, gluing the tiles down with special cork-tile adhesive.

YOU WILL NEED

- ☐ Unsealed cork tiles (see page 23)
- ☐ Floor paint in two colors (see page 23)
- ☐ 1-inch (2.5-cm) paintbrush
- ☐ Cork-tile adhesive
- ☐ Adhesive spreader

CORE TECHNIQUES

- ☐ Flooring (see page 34)

Nature of problem:
concrete floor

Extent of solution:
permanent cure

Finish:
checkered tiles

Time:
4 hours

The problem with cork tiles is that their natural color is a heavy mid-brown. Surprisingly, they take paint well. Choose a hard-wearing floor paint in a color that works with the rest of the room.

GETTING IT RIGHT

Excess adhesive will seep through the joins between the tiles; immediately wipe it off with a damp cloth. You can paint over any stubborn, remaining glue marks once the floor has been laid and the glue has dried.

SOLUTION 2: *Patterned vinyl tiles*

1 Using the compass, mark a circle on a white tile.

3 Without peeling the backings off the tiles, lay them out on the floor in your planned arrangement. When you are happy with the design, set aside the cutout circles in the correct order. Lay all the tiles. Finally, peel the backing off the circles and fit them into the appropriate squares.

2 Using the box cutter, cut out the circle. Score carefully around the pencil lines and then cut over the scored line several times until the circle comes away easily. Use the outer section of the tile as a stencil to draw the same circle onto a black tile. Note that while the circles must be the same size, they don't have to be in the same position on the tiles. Using the tile as your guide ensures that any variations during cutting will be transferred to the other tile, giving a snug fit. Repeat the process, completing all the cutout tiles before laying.

Vary the sizes and positions of the circles on the tiles for the most dramatic effect.

PLAIN black and white vinyl tiles are inexpensive and hard-wearing, but not visually interesting when laid in the conventional way. However, it's very simple to add an extra dimension by cutting out identical circles in a black and a white tile and swapping the cutouts. Take some time to plan your floor beforehand to ensure that you have a balanced arrangement of plain and inlaid tiles and that the circles are in the most advantageous positions.

YOU WILL NEED

☐ Self-adhesive black and white vinyl tiles (see page 23)

☐ Compass

☐ Box cutter

CORE TECHNIQUES

☐ Flooring (see page 34)

Nature of problem:
concrete floor

Extent of solution:
permanent cure

Finish:
patterned tiles

Time:
5 hours

THE PROBLEM: Uneven concrete floor

You can cover a firm, flat concrete floor with almost any flooring material, but when the concrete is uneven or old and flaking, many flooring options disappear. A concrete floor can be re-leveled, but because a professional should do this, it can be an expensive and time-consuming job. The solutions offered here are suitable for floors in almost any state and all of them have the advantage of being inexpensive. Older concrete floors often flake in thin layers and you should remove all loose material before tackling any solution. For a durable finish, always use floor paint for any of the painted finishes.

SOLUTION 1: *Painted faux flagstones*

As with any faux effect, if you copy a real flagstone, your floor will look more realistic. Find a picture and copy the colors and pattern. The original concrete is the perfect texture and color for the cement between the flags. This technique requires little skill and can be finished quite quickly.

YOU WILL NEED

☐ Ruler

☐ Pencil

☐ Floor paints in light, mid and dark stone colors (see page 23)

☐ 2-inch (5-cm) paintbrush

☐ 3-inch (7.5-cm) paintbrush

CORE TECHNIQUES

☐ Painting (see page 24)

Nature of problem:
uneven concrete floor

Extent of solution:
visual disguise

Finish:
painted flagstones

Time:
3 hours

1 Using a pencil and long ruler or a spirit level with marked measurements, draw the flagstones on the concrete. Leave a 1 1/2 inch (4 cm) gap between each one to represent the grout lines.

2 Using a 2-inch (5-cm) paintbrush, paint each flagstone in the dark stone floor paint, making the corners slightly rounded. Brush paint over the surface, ensuring that it's thick along the edges to give each flag a solid edge. Don't try to make the edges perfectly straight; unevenness will add to the effect. Leave to dry.

3 Dip the ends of the bristles of the 3-inch (7.5-cm) paintbrush into the mid-stone floor paint, and roughly brush it in random patches over each flagstone. Never brush paint right up to the edge because that should stay dark to give a three-dimensional effect. Repeat the process with the light stone color, painting fewer, smaller patches.

> **GETTING IT RIGHT**
>
> *This paint effect looks best when you do it quickly and quite roughly. If you get absorbed in tiny detail the finish will lose the spontaneity that makes it realistic.*

The pale color of this floor makes it suitable for rooms that receive little light, but the size of the flagstones makes it inappropriate for a small room.

SOLUTION 2: *Painted faux terra-cotta tiles*

ORIGINAL terra-cotta tiled floors come in a range of sizes, arrangements, and colors. Find a picture in a book or magazine of a floor that suits your room and match up the colors and arrangement for a more authentic finish. The painting technique is exactly the same as for the flagstone floor, but using appropriate terra-cotta–colored paints instead of gray.

YOU WILL NEED

☐ Ruler

☐ Pencil

☐ Floor paints in dark, mid and light terra-cotta colors (see page 23)

☐ 2-inch (5-cm) paintbrush

CORE TECHNIQUES

☐ Painting (see page 24)

Nature of problem: **uneven concrete floor**

Extent of solution: **visual disguise**

Finish: **painted terra-cotta tiles**

Time: **4 hours**

This paint effect is well suited to a smaller room because you can make the tiles almost any size and the multiple grout lines will visually broaden and lengthen the room.

GETTING IT RIGHT

The smaller size of the terra-cotta tiles means that you have to use a 2-inch (5-cm) paintbrush throughout and paint more edges, so this effect will take a little longer than the flagstone floor.

SOLUTION 3: *Broken tiles*

1 Lay the floor using the broken tile method (see page 63) and leave the grout to dry overnight. Following the manufacturer's instructions, spread the grout stain over all of the grouted areas. Don't worry if you get it on the tiles; it will wipe off.

2 Leave the stain for the stated time and then wipe off any excess with a damp cloth.

O N uneven floors ceramic tiles will crack under pressure. To prevent this, break up the tiles: the smaller surface areas aren't subject to such stress. Use the *Broken-tile Tiling* technique (see page 63) to lay the floor. Because there is so much of it, it can be expensive to use colored grout, so use white grout and stain it.

Check the grout from time to time and re-grout the floor if it wears to prevent sharp edges from protruding.

YOU WILL NEED
- ☐ Tiles (see page 23)
- ☐ Hammer
- ☐ Tile adhesive
- ☐ Adhesive spreader
- ☐ White grout
- ☐ Grout float
- ☐ Damp cloth
- ☐ Dry cloth
- ☐ Grout stain

CORE TECHNIQUES
- ☐ Tiling (see page 32)

Nature of problem:
concrete floor

Extent of solution:
permanent cure

Finish:
tiled

Time:
9 hours

Laying broken tiles is time-consuming so it's best to use it on small floor areas, such as a downstairs bathroom.

SOLUTION 4: *Stamped faux mosaic*

For this faux effect, original source material is invaluable. Examples of real mosaic floors are available in museums, books, and magazines. Choose a border design and stamp the center of the floor with a plain mosaic pattern. To make a stamp, trace a design and enlarge it to the right size on a photocopier (see page 168).

YOU WILL NEED

☐ Tracing paper

☐ Pencil

☐ Spray adhesive

☐ High-density foam rubber

☐ Craft knife

☐ White floor paint (see page 23)

☐ Masonry roller

☐ Roller tray

☐ Floor paints in two similar and one contrasting color (see page 23)

☐ 1-inch (2.5-cm) square-ended, flat artist's paintbrush

☐ Large stippling brush

Nature of problem:
uneven concrete floor

Extent of solution:
visual disguise

Finish:
stamped mosaic

Time:
8 hours

1 Paint the entire floor with white floor paint and leave it to dry overnight. Using the 1-inch (2.5-cm) square-ended, flat artist's paintbrush, paint the border stamp with the colored masonry paints. This is the most time-consuming part of the process, and you must do it carefully, making sure that each mosaic square has a coat of paint and that the colors are on the right squares.

3 Once the border is complete, fill in the center of the floor. Using a large stippling brush, stipple the entire stamp with floor paint. Immediately stipple over this with a lighter colored paint, using the same brush. Don't cover the whole stamp with the second coat—apply the paint randomly.

2 Position the stamp over the floor in the right place, and press it down onto the concrete. Being careful not to move it sideways, press the back of the stamp to ensure that all the paint comes into contact with the floor. Carefully lift the stamp straight off the floor in one clean movement. Re-paint the stamp and repeat the process, lining up the end of each new stamp with the previous one to produce an unbroken border.

4 Press the stamp onto the floor in the same way as in Step 2, leaving a consistent gap between the edge of the border and the central floor. Repeat the process until the whole floor is covered.

GETTING IT RIGHT

Once the whole floor is complete and dry, you can go back and tidy up any edges that have bled with the white floor paint.

Creating a stamped mosaic floor design can be time-consuming, so this treatment may not be suitable for large areas. A room with built-in features can also be difficult because you will need to work out the border pattern carefully so you can stamp around them.

SOLUTION 5: *Painted faux slates*

Tʜɪs effect is the perfect solution for an old, flaking concrete floor because the texture replicates the surface of slate. Slate tiles can vary in color from green to gray to black tones. Because they are usually laid in large squares, it's simple to plan the floor. The easiest slate to imitate is a dark gray color.

1 Using the 3-inch (7.5-cm) paintbrush, paint the whole floor with a solid coat of dark gray floor paint and leave to dry overnight. Using a pencil and a long ruler or a spirit level with marked measurements, draw the slates on the floor in a square grid pattern.

2 Dip the tip of the 1-inch (2.5-cm) paintbrush into the dark gray-green paint and dry brush long, straight patches within each marked tile. Work across from the edges, varying the starting points to define the squares. Keep the patches running in the same direction.

YOU WILL NEED

- ☐ Ruler
- ☐ Pencil
- ☐ Floor paints in dark gray, dark gray-green, and light gray (see page 23)
- ☐ Paint can
- ☐ Paint thinner
- ☐ 3-inch (7.5-cm) paintbrush
- ☐ 1-inch (2.5-cm) paintbrush
- ☐ Lining brush

CORE TECHNIQUES

- ☐ Painting (see page 24)

Nature of problem:
flaking concrete floor

Extent of solution:
visual disguise

Finish:
painted slates

Time:
4 hours

3 Once the whole floor is painted and dry, paint in the grout lines. Dilute the light gray floor paint in a paint can with paint thinner until it's the consistency of thin cream. This will make it flow more easily and allow you to paint straighter lines more quickly. Load the lining brush with the diluted paint, lay the ruler or spirit level exactly along the pencil lines, and run the paintbrush along the edge of it.

GETTING IT RIGHT

If the grout lines appear too uneven, finish the whole floor and once it's dry, go back with the base color to make the edges neater.

This effect can be used to turn the worst concrete floor into smart slate in just a few hours—all for the cost of three cans of paint.

THE PROBLEM: Old or stained floorboards

Floorboards are a traditional flooring and are still commonly used, even in new homes. Because they have the potential to be a feature in themselves, you can treat them in many different ways to increase their visual appeal and tie them into a decorative scheme without the expense of changing the flooring.

To an extent the condition of the floorboards dictates the options available. Previous patch-ups may have been mismatched, or the floorboards may be worn and old. The first thing to do is clean them properly to get more of an idea of their possibilities. Start by sanding a patch to see if it's worth stripping them. If it is, rent a floor sander, because it quickly takes off surface layers to reveal smooth, clean boards. This is the best starting point for most of the solutions, though some may not need this initial work.

SOLUTION 1: *Tinted with paint*

Give wood a bleached look with a pale pickling stain. This soaks into wood, so it's suitable for raw boards in reasonable condition. This treatment diminishes the wood grain and makes the overall color more uniform. You apply only one coat, so this is a quick way to treat floorboards.

Brush the pickling stain onto the floor, working along one board at a time and following the direction of the grain. Leave to dry. Seal the floor with two coats of floor varnish or polyurethane.

Test the varnish or polyurethane in an unobtrusive corner first to ensure that it doesn't add a yellow tint to the floor.

YOU WILL NEED

☐ Pickling stain (see page 25)

☐ 2-inch (5-cm) paintbrush

☐ Floor varnish or polyurethane (see page 23)

CORE TECHNIQUES

☐ Painting (see page 24)

Nature of problem:
old floorboards

Extent of solution:
visual enhancement

Finish:
pale boards

Time:
1 hour

SOLUTION 2: *Bleached floorboards*

ORDINARY bleach, the household variety used to clean the kitchen sink, can be used to lighten floorboards that are in basically good condition, but which are rather stained. All previous coverings must be stripped off and the floorboards sanded.

Wearing rubber gloves and working on three or four boards at a time, brush the bleach onto the wood, leave until dry, and then wash over it with lukewarm water and a mop.

This is a very inexpensive and simple solution, but it's a little messy and you need to protect your skin from the bleach.

YOU WILL NEED

☐ Household bleach

☐ 2-inch (5-cm) paintbrush

☐ Rubber gloves

☐ Water

☐ Mop

Nature of problem:
old floorboards

Extent of solution:
visual enhancement

Finish:
pale boards

Time:
4 hours

Once the wood is completely dry, which may take a day, brush on a coat of floor wax following the manufacturer's instructions.

SOLUTION 3: *Painted checks*

THIS solution covers the shabbiest of floorboards. It's also quick and easy because the wood is totally covered and there is no need to strip the boards beforehand. Wash the floorboards to remove dirt and grease, dry them, and prime them before painting. If you use the widths of the planks as the measuring guide, the whole pattern needs little masking.

Measure and mark out the design on the floor. Each large square is three boards wide and the same measurement long. Leave one board as the space between each large square. Mask off the outer edges of the large squares with 1-inch (2.5-cm) masking tape, running each length right across the floor in both directions. This masking forms the smaller squares at the intersecting corners of the large ones. Use the large stippling brush to stipple the paint into the masked squares. Remove the tape and leave to dry. Seal the floor with two coats of floor varnish or polyurethane.

GETTING IT RIGHT

Use a lighter color in the larger squares and a darker color in the smaller ones because this will balance the difference in tones in the overall effect.

YOU WILL NEED

- ☐ Ruler
- ☐ Pencil
- ☐ 1-inch (2.5-cm) masking tape
- ☐ Large stippling brush
- ☐ Floor paint in one base color and two colors for the checks (see page 23)
- ☐ Floor varnish or polyurethane (see page 23)
- ☐ 2-inch (5-cm) paintbrush

CORE TECHNIQUES

- ☐ Painting (see page 24)

Nature of problem:
old floorboards

Extent of solution:
visual enhancement

Finish:
checked boards

Time:
2 hours

This sophisticated effect is extremely easy to achieve and will brighten and freshen up any room.

SOLUTION 4: *Clear varnished floorboards*

Read the directions on the varnish or polyurethane and follow any safety instructions. Ensure that the floor is as dust free and clean as possible. Brush the varnish or polyurethane onto the floorboards, working on one at a time. Use long strokes and follow the direction of the grain. Leave to dry and apply a second coat.

THIS solution allows the floorboards to retain their original appearance. It gives no opportunity for masking or disguising damaged areas, so it's best for floorboards that have been thoroughly sanded and are uniform in color. The floor varnish or polyurethane serves to seal and protect the wood and two coats are normally sufficient for a durable finish.

GETTING IT RIGHT

If you have a large floor, apply the varnish or polyurethane quickly and evenly with a sponge roller. Immediately brush out any small bubbles with a paintbrush, following the direction of the grain.

YOU WILL NEED

☐ Clear floor varnish or polyurethane (see page 23)

☐ 2-inch (5-cm) paintbrush

☐ Sponge roller

☐ Roller tray

Nature of problem:
old floorboards

Extent of solution:
visual enhancement

Finish:
natural boards

Time:
2 hours

Careful sanding will bring old boards up to a good enough standard for a transparent covering.

SOLUTION 5: *Tinted floorboards*

THIS solution offers a way of keeping a natural wood look, but disguising mismatched or badly stained boards. The technique involves building up layers of tinted varnish or polyurethane until the desired depth of color is achieved. Because you apply the varnish with a brush, the streaks you create strengthen the look of the wood grain and help to cover any marks.

Tinted varnish and polyurethane are available in shades from rich mahogany in tones of red to dark walnut with a green-brown finish. Choose a tone that fits into your scheme, bearing in mind that a very dark floor can fight with the color on the walls.

YOU WILL NEED

☐ Tinted varnish or polyurethane (see page 23)

☐ 2-inch (5-cm) paintbrush

Nature of problem:
old floorboards

Extent of solution:
visual enhancement

Finish:
dark wood boards

Time:
1 hour (per coat)

Read the directions on the tin of tinted varnish or polyurethane and follow any safety instructions. Brush the finish onto the floorboards, working along one board at a time using long strokes and following the direction of the grain in the wood. Any brush marks will only add to the effect. Leave to dry then repeat the process until you achieve a shade you like.

> **GETTING IT RIGHT**
>
> *You can use one color of varnish or polyurethane over another to modify the final color, but it's best to test this first on a spare piece of lumber before painting the floor.*

SOLUTION 6: *Masked border*

1 Draw up and mask off the border pattern on the floorboards. Roller a generous coat of liquid masking over the whole border area, including the masking tape.

2 Immediately pull the tape off the floorboards. Wait for the liquid masking to dry.

GETTING IT RIGHT

The masking fluid will completely ruin the gloss roller so don't try to clean it. Just throw it away.

3 Brush the pickling stain over the whole floor in the direction of the grain, covering the liquid masking completely.

T<small>HIS</small> solution is based on the same principle as the tinted floor, but adds a border to create pattern and color. The effect is based on the subtle difference between natural and washed wood surfaces. Liquid masking is a perfect medium for sealing the selected areas that form the border pattern, protecting them from contact with the pickling stain.

4 When the pickling stain on top of the liquid masking is dry, use your fingers to rub it and the hardened fluid off the wood. It will peel away in rubbery strands. If your fingers get sore, try wearing a rubber glove. Once you have removed all of the hardened liquid masking, seal the floor with two coats of floor varnish or polyurethane.

Plan a simple pattern that can be easily reproduced around the room. The plainer the design, the slower it will date.

YOU WILL NEED

- ☐ Masking tape
- ☐ Liquid masking
- ☐ Gloss roller
- ☐ Pickling stain (see page 25)
- ☐ 2-inch (5-cm) paintbrush
- ☐ Floor varnish or polyurethane (see page 23)

Nature of problem:
old floorboards

Extent of solution:
visual enhancement

Finish:
tinted boards with border

Time:
4 hours

THE PROBLEM: Uneven baseboards

There are very few houses, unless brand new, that haven't had some structural modifications—walls removed or extensions added. This invariably affects baseboards. Often the original sizes and profiles could not be found, so mismatched pieces were added or the new baseboards are no longer flush with remaining sections of the originals. You can remove all the baseboards and replace them, but that entails considerable cost and effort. The alternatives offer simple, inexpensive solutions for minimizing the problem by creating a visual distraction or by leveling an obvious misalignment.

SOLUTION 1: *Painted top edge*

A DIFFERENCE in height is the most obvious baseboard problem. The way to overcome it is to distract the eye by painting the baseboard color in a straight line across the wall, in line with the highest point. For particularly bad mismatches paint the baseboards and wall the same color, taking away the eye-catching line completely.

Place one end of the spirit level on the top of the highest baseboard and draw a line over the shorter sections. Run a line of painting tape along the top of the pencil line. Paint the baseboard and the wall below the tape white. Peel off the tape immediately.

> **GETTING IT RIGHT**
>
> *Paint the wall first, then the baseboard. Any areas where the white paint bleeds can be painted over once they are completely dry.*

YOU WILL NEED

☐ Painting tape

☐ Spirit level

☐ 2-inch (5-cm) paintbrush

☐ White eggshell or satin paint (see page 23)

CORE TECHNIQUES

☐ Painting (see page 24)

Nature of problem: **uneven top edge**

Extent of solution: **visual disguise**

Finish: **painted edge**

Time: **2 hours**

Against a colored wall this white, straight band will look even, though the profiles cannot be made to align.

SOLUTION 2: *Scarfed-in baseboard*

1 Wrap the sandpaper around the wooden block, stapling it at the back if necessary to keep it in place. Sand across the join between the two baseboards, sanding

the raised edge until the two edges are as even as possible. Keep the sanding block parallel to the baseboards so that you don't dig into the shallower one.

2 To protect the floor, stick a length of painting tape beneath the area to be filled. Following the manufacturer's instructions, mix up some epoxy filler. Using the filler knife,

smooth filler over the join, leveling out any remaining discrepancies between the two baseboards. Leave to dry completely.

EVEN when the identical profile was used, patched sections of baseboard are not always flush. The baseboard itself may be thicker or the wall may be slightly out of line where a new section was plastered. Scarfing, or making a smooth join, is quite labor-intensive, but the final result can be almost invisible.

3 Sand the filler smooth, paying particular attention to the molding at the top of the baseboard. Clean up any dust and paint the baseboard.

GETTING IT RIGHT

When you are filling the join, smooth the filler as much as possible with the knife so that you have a minimum of sanding. If there is still a slight depression once you have sanded, apply a little more filler and repeat the process.

The only sign that these baseboards were once uneven is that they don't run straight along the floor. Other than that the join is now invisible.

YOU WILL NEED

- ☐ 120-grit sandpaper
- ☐ Wooden sanding block
- ☐ Painting tape
- ☐ Epoxy filler
- ☐ Filler knife
- ☐ 2-inch (5-cm) paintbrush
- ☐ White eggshell or satin paint (see page 23)

CORE TECHNIQUES

- ☐ Painting (see page 24)

Nature of problem:
uneven profile

Extent of solution:
permanent cure

Finish:
smooth join

Time:
2 hours

THE PROBLEM: **Worn or stained carpet**

When you buy a home you often inherit fixtures and fittings chosen by somebody else, invariably some years ago. Carpet is a prime example. New carpet can be expensive, especially because you have to hire a professional fitter to lay enormous lengths well. If the existing carpet is acceptable and your budget is more urgently required elsewhere, it's best to just tidy it up.

However, if you do have to remove the existing carpet, you can replace it with carpet tiles that you can lay yourself.

SOLUTION I: *Cleaned and covered*

OLD carpet invariably bears the scars of time, from built-up dirt to accidental spills. Professional cleaning services are available but it's less expensive to rent a carpet-cleaner and do it yourself. The results can be quite dramatic and can prolong the life of the carpet by years. The worst areas are often near furniture where food or drinks have made immovable stains. Fortunately these are also the places where you can use decorative rugs to cover problems.

YOU WILL NEED

☐ Carpet-cleaning machine

☐ Area rugs

Nature of problem:
damaged carpet

Extent of solution:
physical disguise

Finish:
rugs

Time:
2 hours

Choose rugs to match the furniture in the room rather than the existing carpet. When you do replace the carpet, you can still use the rugs.

SOLUTION 2: *Carpet tiles*

CARPET tiles are so small and easy to handle that you can lay them yourself on either wooden or concrete floors. In addition, you can replace tiles that become damaged or stained, so they are an ideal solution for kitchens or children's rooms. The tiles have directional arrows on the back. To ensure that the nap goes in the same direction, lay them with the arrows pointing the same way. Stick carpet tape to every edge of each tile and a strip across the middle. Press them firmly into position.

YOU WILL NEED
☐ Carpet tiles
☐ Carpet tape

Nature of problem:
damaged carpet

Extent of solution:
permanent cure

Finish:
carpet tiles

Time:
4 hours

Carpet tiles are available in a range of colors, so you might think of creating a checkerboard or border pattern. However, the quality of the tiles isn't usually good enough to warrant any emphasis, so neutral colors are safest.

OF THE THREE major surfaces in a room, ceilings hold the least visual presence and often get little attention. They are generally painted white, either due to the visual problems of using color or because treating the surface is rarely more than an afterthought. However, if they are totally neglected, the overall appearance of the room can be seriously compromised. Investing a bit of time and effort on the ceiling will help to create a finished look.

There are two main problems normally encountered with ceilings: the actual surface and the join between the ceiling and wall. Because working on ceilings is hard and extremely tiring, the solutions are quick and simple. As with most decorative problems, there are two main types of solution—those that offer a physical change and those that disguise or distract from the problem. Whether you have an older home that has been poorly modernized or a modern apartment, you will find an appropriate solution to ceiling problems in the pages that follow.

ceilings

The problem: Uneven ceiling to wall join

This problem can appear in all types of buildings, but is far more common in older houses that have been subject to even a little movement over a long time.

If the wall was painted up to the ceiling line—the usual way of painting a ceiling and wall—the uneven wall to ceiling join would be emphasized. By moving the joining line onto either the ceiling itself or down onto the wall, you take attention away from the problem while also changing the visual dimension of the room to suit the space.

SOLUTION 1: *Painted line on ceiling*

IF the room is low, take the paint line up onto the ceiling. This adds visual height and disguises the uneven join. A spirit level won't work on the ceiling, so you have to assume that the wall is level and measure a band about 4 inches (10 cm) deep from that. Painting tape doesn't sit flat on textured ceilings, so hand-paint the edge.

1 Paint the whole ceiling. Using the try-square, measure from the wall to the desired depth and make a pencil mark on the ceiling. Repeat at 20-inch (50-cm) intervals along the wall. Join the marks using a ruler and pencil.

2 Paint the wall up to the ceiling. Then carefully paint along the pencil line and fill in the color back to the wall.

YOU WILL NEED

☐ Try-square

☐ Pencil

☐ Long ruler

☐ Matte latex paint in two colors (see page 23)

☐ 4-inch (10-cm) paintbrush

CORE TECHNIQUES

☐ Painting (see page 24)

Nature of problem:
uneven join

Extent of solution:
visual disguise

Finish:
colored band

Time:
3 hours

GETTING IT RIGHT

The easiest way to achieve a straight edge over a rough surface is to brush the paint in both directions several times until it looks even. If the wall color spreads over the wrong side of the pencil line, wait until it's dry and paint over the mistake with the ceiling color.

A fairly pale wall color is best for this technique because a strong color reaching onto the ceiling can make the room look smaller.

SOLUTION 2: *Painted line on wall*

1 Paint the ceiling and the top section of the wall. Because the ceiling to wall line is uneven and it's unlikely that the ceiling is level, take just one measurement down from the ceiling to the desired depth of the band. Using a spirit level, mark a straight line around the room.

2 Mask above the line with painting tape. Brush paint up to the taped line, using random brushstrokes for a lightly mottled effect. Peel off the tape.

IF the room has a tall ceiling, but you would like a more cozy, intimate feeling, you can visually lower the ceiling by dropping the line of ceiling color down onto the wall. You can vary the depth according to how high the ceiling is, but it should be at least 4 inches (10 cm) to look intentional and distract the eye.

A panel in a contrasting color that breaks through the painted line and reaches the ceiling adds another element to this solution.

YOU WILL NEED

☐ Ruler

☐ Spirit level

☐ Pencil

☐ Painting tape

☐ Matte latex paint in two colors (see page 23)

☐ 3-inch (7.5-cm) paintbrush

CORE TECHNIQUES

☐ Painting (see page 24)

Nature of problem:
uneven join

Extent of solution:
visual disguise

Finish:
white band

Time:
2 hours

The problem: Textured or damaged ceiling

To avoid the effort and expense of replastering ceilings that are uneven, cracked, or have an existing textured, papered, or plastered finish, either flatten the existing texture or add more. Ceilings covered in textured paper or with raised patterns can be leveled to create a softer surface. A damaged ceiling can be given a more desirable, consistent texture that simultaneously covers all the faults.

SOLUTION 1: *Rough plaster effect*

USE a technique similar to plastering to improve an unattractive textured ceiling. The principle is the same as that used in the *Lightly Textured Top Coat* (see page 50), but gravity will be working against you this time. To control the textured covering and avoid a terrible mess, work in small sections.

YOU WILL NEED

- ☐ Textured covering (see page 23)
- ☐ 4-inch (10-cm) paintbrush
- ☐ Grout float
- ☐ Masonry roller
- ☐ Roller tray
- ☐ Matte latex paint (see page 23)

CORE TECHNIQUES

- ☐ Adding texture (see page 30)

Nature of problem:
textured ceiling

Extent of solution:
permanent cure

Finish:
light texture

Time:
7 hours

1 Work in easy-to-manage sections, approximately 1-foot (30-cm) square, across the ceiling. Using the paintbrush, paint the textured covering thickly onto the ceiling, brushing it out to form an even layer.

2 Hold a grout float at an angle so that only the long side edge is in contact with the ceiling. Lightly smooth over the textured covering with long, sweeping strokes. Don't try to make the surface perfectly smooth—the irregularities are part of the effect.

Leave the ceiling to dry overnight and then use a masonry roller to paint it with latex paint. Because the surface is highly absorbent, it needs the paint to seal it. Therefore, always apply two coats of paint, even if the color looks solid after one coat.

Here the ceiling wasn't only covered with textured paper, the wall to ceiling line was also uneven. The ceiling line was dropped onto the wall (see page 93), but the texture was confined to the ceiling only.

SOLUTION 2: *Papered with handmade paper*

Following the manufacturer's instructions, mix up the wallpaper paste. Working on one sheet of paper at a time, use the 4-inch (10-cm) paintbrush to apply the paste to the back of the paper. Stick the sheet of paper to the ceiling and brush over it with the dry 3-inch (7.5-cm) paintbrush.

HEAVILY textured surfaces are unsuitable for papering so this solution is more successful on ceilings that have light damage, cracks, or are uneven. Because handmade paper is available only in sheets, pasting it to the ceiling can be done without the usual problems associated with wallpapering. Depending on the paper you choose, this can be a relatively expensive solution. It may be best suited to a smaller room.

YOU WILL NEED

☐ Wallpaper paste
☐ Paint can
☐ Sheets of handmade paper (see page 23)
☐ 4-inch (10-cm) paintbrush
☐ 3-inch (7.5-cm) paintbrush

CORE TECHNIQUES

☐ Wallpapering (see page 31)

Nature of problem: **damaged ceiling**

Extent of solution: **permanent cure**

Finish: **papered**

Time: **3 hours**

You can choose from a wide variety of papers with textures, inlaid motifs, and colors. The general rule is to keep it light, plain, and natural; otherwise, the ceiling may feel low and become overbearing.

GETTING IT RIGHT

Start in one corner and work outward, butting one piece tight against the next. If the paper needs to be cut down, measure and lightly mark the right size. Hold a ruler firmly in place at the marked point and tear the paper along it to keep a handmade edge.

The problem: **No cornice**

The cornice is a decorative device at the top of the wall, disguising the join between the walls and ceiling. It also serves as a frame, making the top edges of the wall appear crisp and neat. Cornices are usually only found in older homes, but they fit perfectly well into modern interiors. If your room doesn't have a cornice and you want the decorative detail it offers, you can add one, or you can use paint to create a similar effect.

SOLUTION 1: *Fitting a cornice*

CORNICES come in a range of materials, depths, styles, and prices. The more expensive ones are made of plaster and are more decorative and deeper. However, they are rigid and can be fitted only on level walls. So if the walls are uneven, you'll achieve a better fit with a cheaper polystyrene molding.

YOU WILL NEED

☐ Polystyrene cornice
☐ Tape measure
☐ Pencil
☐ Miter block
☐ Backsaw
☐ Project glue
☐ Thin nails
☐ Hammer
☐ 2-inch (10-cm) paintbrush
☐ Matte latex paint (see page 23)

CORE TECHNIQUES

☐ Painting (see page 24)

Nature of problem:
no cornice

Extent of solution:
permanent cure

Finish:
simple cornice

Time:
4 hours

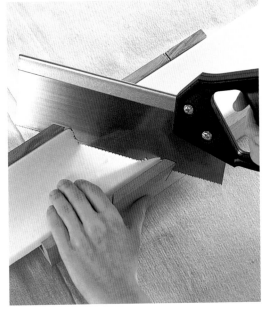

1 Start working from one corner of the room. Measure the length of the wall and cut the molding to size. Use a miter block to cut the ends at 45 degrees to make neat, mitered corners.

2 Run a wavy line of adhesive along both back sides of the molding. Place it against the wall and push it firmly into place.

3 Hammer in nails above and below the molding at intervals to hold it in place while the adhesive dries. Continue around the room, ensuring that where square ends meet in a length of wall, they sit together with a flush profile. Paint the molding with two coats of latex paint.

> **GETTING IT RIGHT**
>
> *Use the molding in as long lengths as possible. The fewer joins there are along a wall, the neater it looks and the easier it is to achieve a good finish.*

A plain molding is easy to fit and will suit a traditionally styled or contemporary room.

SOLUTION 2: *Painted band*

To create the impression of a cornice, paint a simple band of white. This is a good solution for rooms with very uneven ceiling to wall joins that would make fitting molding difficult. The only rule is that the ceiling must be painted a color; it doesn't have to be the same as the wall, but it can't be white. Choose a light color to avoid making the ceiling feel lower, but it must contrast enough with white to make the line apparent.

Paint the ceiling and wall the correct colors with the roller. Using the paintbrush, paint the approximate area of the band white. Working from the wall to ceiling join, measure and mark the same distance out onto the ceiling and down onto the wall. Use a spirit level to draw a straight line on the wall. On the ceiling repeat the measurement at regular points, and join the marks with a ruler and pencil. Pour some ceiling paint into the roller tray, dip the paint pad into it, and remove the excess on the edge of the tray. Pull the pad along the ceiling, following the drawn line. Paint the rest of the ceiling. Repeat the process on the wall.

YOU WILL NEED

☐ Long-pile roller

☐ Roller tray

☐ 2-inch (10-cm) paintbrush

☐ Matte latex paint in two colors and white (see page 23)

☐ Ruler

☐ Pencil

☐ 8-inch (20-cm) paint pad

CORE TECHNIQUES

☐ Painting (see page 24)

Nature of problem:
no cornice

Extent of solution:
visual enhancement

Finish:
painted band

Time:
3 hours

The stronger the colors, the greater the visual impact but only tall, well-lit rooms can take strong ceiling colors.

SOLUTION 3: *Painted border*

Using a spirit level as described in *Painted Rectangles* (see page 42), draw a series of small rectangles around the top of the wall. The largest should be the depth of the border you want—10 inches (25 cm) is usually a good depth. Draw them in randomly arranged, overlapping groups of three that consist of one large rectangle, one long, thin one, and one small one. Using the flat, square-ended paintbrush, paint the largest in the light color, the thin one in the dark color, and the smallest in the pearlized paint, in that order.

To approach the problem from a totally different angle, choose a bold yet simple pattern and add a wide decorative border. The spirit level gives a positioning guide, and the flat, square-ended paintbrush produces crisp corners. The walls and ceiling in the room must be painted the same light base color, or the ceiling to wall join will distract from the border.

YOU WILL NEED

- ☐ Spirit level
- ☐ 1-inch (2.5-cm) square-ended, flat paintbrush
- ☐ Matte latex paints in a light and a dark, accent color (see page 23)
- ☐ Pearlized paint (see page 23)

CORE TECHNIQUES

- ☐ Painting (see page 24)

Nature of problem:
no cornice

Extent of solution:
visual enhancement

Finish:
painted pattern

Time:
4 hours

Because the effect is strong, and the process involves judging by eye and freehand painting, this technique is suitable for adventurous painters even though the right tools make it relatively quick and simple.

OPEN PLAN LIVING is the trend these days, but there are certain rooms that will always need doors, most obviously bathrooms and bedrooms. Unsympathetic modernization can leave an older house with inappropriate doors, but replacing them can be an expensive option. If your doors work efficiently and have no major damage, try decorating them instead. If your doors are mismatched and you want them to be the same, flat, plain versions are the cheapest on the market so even when not bought in bulk they are probably still the best budget choice.

This chapter provides permanent solutions that utilize existing plain doors. There are a range of solutions, varying in their levels of decoration and complexity, but all are achievable with no special skills. There are quick and easy simple embellishments for a decorative or a practical approach and solutions that involve simple paint effects.

This chapter also deals with other common problems: a damaged door and a short door when carpet is removed. Again, the emphasis is on treating the existing door, as opposed to having it replaced.

A good way to spruce up old doors is to buy attractive door handles. Finding ones that are different, dramatic, or just a little bit special will make a world of difference to the final look.

doors

THE PROBLEM: **A flat door**

The cheapest and therefore most commonly used types of doors are the flat variety with no panels or molding. These doors serve their function perfectly well but can look plain and inappropriate, especially in older homes. There are a number of ways in which you can visually enhance them or integrate them into a room's decorating scheme. Decorating your doors has other advantages, too. You can match all the doors in a foyer, for example, and on the other sides, decorate them to suit the scheme of the other rooms. This solves the problem of having to find one style that fits all, which will invariably require a compromise somewhere. Any original surface will need to be keyed and primed appropriately before painting.

SOLUTION 1: *A blackboard door*

A VERY simple and easy to achieve way to make a plain door more attractive is to give it a further function. A blackboard painted onto the face of the door can provide useful memo space in a kitchen or study and is even more fun in a child's bedroom or playroom. Blackboard paint is inexpensive, readily available, and can be applied straight over the existing paint or surface on the door.

2 Paint the masked-off panel with blackboard paint, brushing it on smoothly and evenly, so that the surface is as flat as possible. Remove the tape immediately and leave to dry.

YOU WILL NEED

☐ Eggshell paint (see page 23)

☐ 1-inch (2.5-cm) paintbrush

☐ Pencil

☐ Ruler

☐ Painting tape

☐ Blackboard paint

CORE TECHNIQUES

☐ Painting (see page 24)

Nature of problem:
flat door

Extent of solution:
visual enhancement

Finish:
blackboard

Time:
30 minutes

1 Paint the door with two coats of eggshell paint in the background color and leave to dry. Measure and draw out the blackboard panel, which can be as large or as small as you wish. Mask off the edges with painting tape.

GETTING IT RIGHT

Keep a dry cloth or a blackboard eraser to hand remove light chalk marks, and periodically wipe over the whole blackboard with a damp cloth to clean the surface completely.

To keep the chalk handy, fix a right-angle length of molding across the bottom of the blackboard with project glue to make a narrow shelf.

SOLUTION 2: *Trompe l'oeil wooden panels*

IF YOUR heart is set on having solid wood doors but your budget says definitely not, then here is the answer. By using tinted varnish in realistic wood tones you can easily imitate the arrangement of the panels in wooden doors. This is a simple faux effect you can achieve and it won't require any special brushes.

1 Base coat the door with white eggshell paint and leave to dry. Plan the arrangement of panels on the door: a good effect can be gained with a 4-inch (10-cm) wide strip running up each side of the door, another

at the top and bottom and one just above the middle of the door. Measure and mark out the panels. Tape off the two central panels created by marking out the strips. Using a 2-inch (5-cm) paintbrush, brush the varnish onto the panels in long, smooth strokes, each stroke running from top to bottom of the panel. While the varnish is still wet, push the brush back through the varnish, bristles first. The bristles at the sides will splay out and help to create an uneven grain.

YOU WILL NEED

☐ White eggshell paint (see page 23)

☐ Pencil

☐ Ruler

☐ Painting tape

☐ Quick-drying tinted varnish in medium oak (see page 23)

☐ 2-inch (5-cm) paintbrush

☐ 1-inch (2.5-cm) paintbrush

CORE TECHNIQUES

☐ Painting (see page 24)

Nature of problem:
flat door

Extent of solution:
visual enhancement

Finish:
faux panels

Time:
2 hours

GETTING IT RIGHT

If you feel that the grain you have created is too strong, simply apply another coat of the varnish, brushing it on flat in the direction of the created grain.

2 Drag the brush lightly back over the wet varnish making sharp stops and starts to create more faux grain. Remove the tape immediately.

3 Put a length of tape across the ends of the shorter panels at the top and bottom of the door and the middle panel. Using the 1-inch (2.5-cm) paintbrush, brush the varnish across the panel, allowing it to overlap the edges of the upper and lower panels. This overlap will create a shadow line. Push the bristles up through the varnish and then create grain as before.

4 Finally, work on the long strips on either side of the door. Using the 1-inch (2.5-cm) paintbrush, brush the varnish on from top to bottom, slightly overlapping the edges of the central panels as before. Push the bristles up through the varnish and then create grain as before.

This traditional style door can be created in any color wood by using different tinted varnishes.

SOLUTION 3: *Faux leather panel*

THIS traditional door, with its rich, dark colors, would fit perfectly in a study or den or in a more formal foyer. The size of the central panel is a subjective decision but a good rule to follow is to have a deeper outer band at the bottom of the door than at the top. The tinted wood varnishes provide a balanced shade for the outer section and burnt umber oil paint is an accurate tone for dark leather. You can make the leather a richer color by making the base redder.

1 Base coat the whole door with salmon-pink eggshell paint and leave to dry. Measure and draw out the central panel and mask it off with painting tape. Working in small sections and using the 2-inch (5-cm) paintbrush, roughly brush on a thick layer of the same pink paint and then stipple it with the tip of the paintbrush to create a thick, dimpled texture. Cover the whole panel in this way. Remove the tape immediately and leave to dry.

2 At the top and bottom of the door place lengths of tape running from the edge of the painted panel to the end of the door. Using the 2-inch (5-cm) paintbrush, apply two coats of varnish, brushing across the width of the door. Each brushstroke should run right across the taped section. Varnish right up to the edge of the painted panel.

Remove the tape and brush two coats of varnish onto the side sections of the door, using long, smooth brushstrokes. There is no need to tape the sides, but try not to overlap the short varnished sections.

3 When the varnish is completely dry, re-tape the central panel. Using the stippling brush, stipple the artist's oil paint over the whole panel, ensuring that it's worked into all the crevices in the pink paint.

4 Immediately rub the excess paint off the panel with a soft cloth. Where the texture is heavier more of the burnt umber will be removed, giving a leathery effect. Leave to dry completely; this can take up to three days.

The upholstery tacks define the two textures and add a sense of realism because they are usually used to edge real leather.

YOU WILL NEED

☐ Salmon-pink eggshell paint (see page 23)

☐ 2-inch (5-cm) paintbrush

☐ Pencil

☐ Ruler

☐ Painting tape

☐ Quick-drying tinted varnish in walnut (see page 23)

☐ Burnt umber artist's oil paint

☐ Small stippling brush

☐ Soft cloth

☐ Upholstery tacks in strips

☐ Hammer

CORE TECHNIQUES

☐ Painting (see page 24)

| Nature of problem: **flat door** |
| Extent of solution: **visual enhancement** |
| Finish: **faux leather panel** |
| Time: **4 hours** |

GETTING IT RIGHT

It doesn't matter if you get a little varnish onto the painted center section as the artist's oil color will cover it. If you are worried about overlapping the top and bottom varnished sections when varnishing the sides, wait for the top and bottom to dry and then mask them off before varnishing the sides.

5 Starting in one corner and following the manufacturer's instructions, hammer a line of upholstery tacks right around the central panel.

SOLUTION 4: *Raised panels*

RATHER than adding texture or color, you can create a three-dimensional surface, adding profile to the door. This is an extremely easy solution to achieve, and if you don't have a jigsaw, ask your lumber supplier to cut the medium density fiberboard to size for you.

1 Base coat the door with one coat of eggshell paint, and leave to dry. Measure and mark out the size and positions of the panels on the door.

2 Measure, mark, and cut out MDF panels the same size as the drawn panels on the door.

YOU WILL NEED

☐ Eggshell paint (see page 23)

☐ 1-inch (2.5-cm) paintbrush

☐ Pencil

☐ Ruler

☐ ⅛-inch (3-mm) thick MDF

☐ Jigsaw

☐ Project glue

☐ Primer

☐ Sandpaper

CORE TECHNIQUES

☐ Painting (see page 24)

Nature of problem:
flat door

Extent of solution:
physical enhancement

Finish:
raised panels

Time:
1½ hours

3 Apply project glue to the back of each panel in turn, and stick it in place.

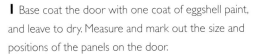

4 Sand the edges of the MDF smooth. Prime and then paint the panels. Finally give the whole door a second coat of paint.

GETTING IT RIGHT

If you are unsure as to how to place the panels on the door to best suit your room, cut pieces of thick card to size and tape them on the painted door with masking tape. When you are happy with the arrangement, draw around the panels and then follow the solution from step 2.

The design of the paneling on this door is modern and minimal but it can be as simple or as complex as you wish.

THE PROBLEM: Damaged or short door

Daily wear and tear and damage from feet and pets most commonly occurs at the base of a door. Filling and repainting the door at a fraction of the cost of replacement can repair this but if the door is subjected to continuous damage, a solution that offers permanent protection is needed.

Another common door problem occurs when carpet is removed in favor of traditional floorboards. The door was hung to the level of the carpet and now it's too short. However, if the room the door opens into is still carpeted, then you cannot alter the door or it won't open properly.

SOLUTION 1: *Metal panel*

THIS solution can be used for short and damaged doors. Ask the metal supplier to cut the aluminum to size.

For a damaged door get a panel 10 inches (25 cm) high by the width of the door minus 2 inches (5 cm). Attach this 1 inch (2.5 cm) above the bottom with contact adhesive.

For a short door, get a panel 12 inches (30 cm) deep and the full width of the door. Attach it so that it overlaps the bottom of the door, hiding the shortfall.

YOU WILL NEED

☐ Brushed aluminum cut to size

☐ Contact adhesive

Nature of problem:
damaged door

Extent of solution:
permanent cure

Finish:
metal

Time:
10 minutes

Metal sheet is available in different finishes, including brushed and polished aluminum, so choose the one that best suits your room.

SOLUTION 2: *Extended baseboard*

A SIMPLE approach to bridging a gap between the door and floor is to continue the baseboard across the door. Cut it to size so that when it's glued on it aligns with the top of the baseboard on either side of the door and just overlaps the bottom of the door, hiding the shortfall. Stick the baseboard to the door with project glue.

For this solution the door must be quite flush with the wall, as a deep recess will cause the new baseboard to jam against the molding and stop the door from opening.

This door is in a junction room (see page 156) so the door has been painted to match the walls.

YOU WILL NEED

☐ Baseboard cut
   to size

☐ Project glue

Nature of problem:
short door

Extent of solution:
physical enhancement

Finish:
extended baseboard

Time:
30 minutes

NATURAL LIGHT IS ONE OF the most important elements in any room. Windows are designed to supply light, but like any other element in a room, they can have problems.

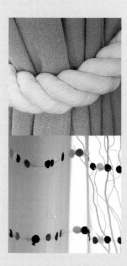

Many of us live in built-up areas where the close proximity of other buildings can mean that you look into someone else's room or the view from the window is less than attractive. Fortunately, you can deal with these issues in several different ways depending on the sort of view you have and the degree of privacy you need.

The other problem that most people experience at one time or another is window treatments, particularly if they are on a budget. Curtains and drapes are expensive to buy and can be difficult to make unless you are very good with a needle. However, there are some clever low-sew and no-sew solutions in this chapter to suit different styles of window.

To allow the maximum amount of natural light into a room, ensure that the curtain rod is wider than the window so that you can pull the curtains or drapes right back. Tie them back during the day to gain as much light as possible: you'll find two simple tieback solutions in this chapter, too.

windows

THE PROBLEM: **An unattractive view or patterned glass**

Windows are often a focal point in a room, but only the most fortunate have the pleasure of looking out onto a wonderful view. Most of us have a less appealing outlook. If you do have an unattractive view, don't totally cover the glass and cut out your natural light as well. Instead, add decorative features to the glass and frame to draw attention away from the view and toward the window itself.

If you don't want to work on the window glass, have a sheet of clear plastic cut to size, decorate it, and fix it into the window frame with clear silicon sealant. It won't be obvious and you can easily remove it at a later date if you wish.

Anti-theft screens and patterned glass present their own problems, both of which can by solved by using color as a distraction.

SOLUTION 1: *Painted glass*

PATTERNED glass helps to ensure privacy while letting in light, but it is often unattractive and dated in appearance. Replacing it with a different pattern can be expensive and result in only a slight improvement. Instead, add colorful decoration to the glass to distract from the pattern.

2 Use two or three colors to paint the stripes of visible glass. Paint the stripes on both sides of a length of tape and immediately peel off the tape. Work across the glass, painting and peeling.

YOU WILL NEED

- ☐ Masking tape in different widths
- ☐ Water-based glass paints
- ☐ Sable paintbrushes, one for each color

CORE TECHNIQUES

- ☐ Painting (see page 24)

Nature of problem:
patterned glass

Extent of solution:
visual disguise

Finish:
painted bands

Time:
2 hours

1 Always work on the smooth side of the glass. Use masking tape to mask off the frame around the glass, then create a pattern of stripes by sticking different widths of tape to the glass, working from the sides inward. Ensure that the first lengths of tape are parallel to the frame and that the subsequent lengths are parallel to each other.

GETTING IT RIGHT

When you are taping the glass, remember that it is the gaps that make the final pattern, not the strips of tape, which are peeled off to reveal clear glass. Work from both sides of the glass into the middle to create a symmetrical pattern, as we have done here, or from one side to the other to create a random pattern. If the paint bleeds under the tape, wait until it's dry before carefully scraping it off with the tip of a craft knife.

Patterned glass is often used in doors as well as windows, and this solution works equally well on both.

SOLUTION 2: *Lead strip and frosting spray*

THIS is a particularly good solution when the view is bad and the window is plain. The strong lines created by the lead strips add detail and make the window a bold, decorative addition to the room. The self-adhesive lead is quite rigid and doesn't curve very well, so plan the design with straight lines.

1 Using a pencil and ruler, draw a simple template on the card; an arrangement of straight lines works well with lead strip. Stick the template to the back of the sheet of plastic or the back of the window with masking tape.

2 Mask off the areas to be frosted with masking tape.

GETTING IT RIGHT

If you are creating the design on a sheet of plastic that will be sealed into the window frame, make sure you clean the glass thoroughly before covering it with the plastic.

3 Lay paper over the rest of the window because the frosting spray tends to drift. Working in a well-ventilated room and following the instructions on the can, spray the masked areas with frosting spray. Carefully peel off the the masking tape and leave to dry.

YOU WILL NEED

- ☐ Pencil
- ☐ Ruler
- ☐ Card cut to the size of the window
- ☐ Rigid plastic cut to the size of the window (optional)
- ☐ Masking tape
- ☐ Paper
- ☐ Frosting spray
- ☐ ⅛-inch (3-mm) and ¼-inch (6-mm) self-adhesive lead strip
- ☐ Scissors
- ☐ Craft knife

Nature of problem: **unattractive view**

Extent of solution: **visual distraction**

Finish: **raised and frosted pattern**

Time: **2 hours**

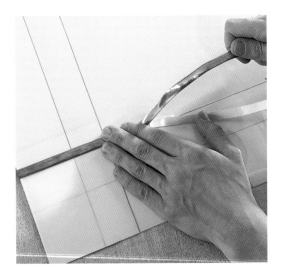

4 Working on the lines that border the frosted areas, cut off slightly more of the ¼-inch (6-mm) lead than you need for a single line. Peel off a section of backing paper and press one end of the lead down onto the glass. Peel off more of the backing and stick down the rest of the strip, following the line on the template. Repeat the process on the other appropriate lines.

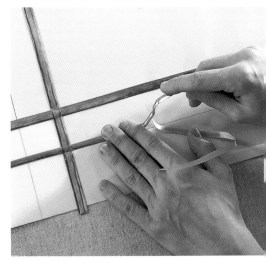

5 Working in the same way, stick the ⅛-inch (3-mm) lead to the remaining lines in the design in the same way, laying it over the thick strips of lead and pressing it down around the overlap with your fingers. ▶

You can alter the design to suit your own window. Experiment by drawing designs onto tracing paper with a thick black pen and sticking them into the window frame to get an impression of the final effect.

6 Use a craft knife to trim off any excess lead at the sides of the glass.

SOLUTION 3: *Patterns with silver leaf*

Large squares of silver leaf on a window can cover a great portion of an unpleasant view. Because the leaf is light-reflective, it bounces light into the room, as well as offering a decorative distraction.

1 Draw a template of the design you want onto the card; here there are three squares in a line down the center of the glass. Tape this to the back of the sheet of plastic or the back of the window.

3 Spray a generous coat of adhesive onto the exposed glass.

YOU WILL NEED

☐ Card cut to the same size as the window
☐ Pencil
☐ Ruler
☐ Piece of plastic cut to the size of the window (optional)
☐ Painting tape
☐ Spray adhesive
☐ 3 sheets of metal transfer leaf
☐ Soft cloth

Nature of problem:
unattractive view

Extent of solution:
visual distraction

Finish:
metal leaf patterns

Time:
I hour

GETTING IT RIGHT

● Peel the backing away slowly, bit by bit. If a lot of the leaf is still attached, carefully put it back down in the same position and rub until it adheres to the surface.

● If you want a different design, lay a stencil on the glass and spray over it with the adhesive. Lay a sheet of leaf over the glue and rub it. Peel off the backing and then use a soft brush to brush away any excess leaf, revealing the design. This technique works best with fairly simple designs because detail can get lost in the process.

2 Mask off the design with painting tape. It is important to mask off all of the glass that isn't being decorated because the spray adhesive tends to drift.

4 Lay a sheet of metal transfer leaf over the sprayed area. Rub the paper backing with a soft cloth to ensure that all the leaf has stuck to the surface and then very carefully peel off the backing. Peel off the painting tape.

Squares work well in a contemporary setting, but you can use a stencil to create almost any simple design.

SOLUTION 4: *Beaded screen*

Many urban dwellers use anti-theft screens on their windows. On larger windows these often take the form of exterior bars, but heavy-duty, interior wire screens are often used on small first floor or basement windows. This solution offers a way to turn an ugly screen into a decorative object. Choose translucent, colored glass in various shapes and sizes and use the grid of the screen to design a pattern. Thread each bead with a length of fine wire, or wrap the wire around the nuggets. Wire them to the grid in your chosen pattern. Trim off any excess wire with pliers.

YOU WILL NEED

☐ Silver beading wire

☐ Glass beads and nuggets in various shapes, sizes, and colors

☐ Pliers

Nature of problem:
patterned glass

Extent of solution:
visual disguise

Finish:
decorated screen

Time:
4 hours

The soft colors of translucent glass will glow as the light comes through the window.

GETTING IT RIGHT

Add the larger beads first in a symmetrical pattern and work outward from these points to quickly and easily build up a balanced effect.

SOLUTION 5: *Patterns with glass painting outliner*

WHEN you want only a light decorative element, the popular craft of glass painting offers a subtle solution. Use the glass painting outliner to draw patterns on the window. The tubes of outliner have a thin nozzle that produces a fine line, so the amount of light won't be affected, and bold motifs won't be overwhelming. A simple approach is to trace over a wallpaper border design or for larger windows, a piece of wallpaper.

GETTING IT RIGHT

Always squeeze the tube of outliner from the bottom and fold the end over as the tube empties. If you make a mistake, leave the outliner to dry, then cut off the section of outliner with the mistake in it with a craft knife and re-draw the line.

Place the patterned paper under the piece of plastic or tape it to the back of the window. Using the wallpaper border as a template, outline elements of the design onto the glass. Leave to dry.

Glass outliner is available in a wide range of colors and metallic finishes, but choose with care. Light colors and silver don't show up well on windows.

YOU WILL NEED

- ☐ Piece of plastic cut to the size of the window (optional)
- ☐ Masking tape
- ☐ Patterned paper
- ☐ Glass outliner

Nature of problem:
unattractive view

Extent of solution:
visual distraction

Finish:
outlined patterns

Time:
30 minutes

THE PROBLEM: Lack of privacy

Rooms such as bedrooms and bathrooms require a degree of privacy but, like any room, especially if it is small, they also need as much light as possible. Sheer curtains are an obvious option, but they don't always suit the style of the room and sometimes don't offer enough privacy. The solutions here offer different levels of privacy, from partial to total, while still letting light into the room.

SOLUTION 1: *Pattern with frosting spray*

THE matte-white, translucent finish of frosting spray allows the original level of light into the room and can also form patterns on the glass. The result can be highly decorative and offer a good amount of privacy, perfectly suited to a bedroom window. Use a template to form the pattern. It will be the negative part of the pattern, the part that is clear glass.

YOU WILL NEED

☐ Tracing paper cut to the size of the window

☐ Spray adhesive

☐ Pencil

☐ Scissors

☐ Frosting spray

Nature of problem:
lack of privacy

Extent of solution:
partial privacy

Finish:
frosted pattern

Time:
2 hours

2 Immediately peel the tracing paper off the glass to reveal the sprayed, negative pattern.

1 Lightly coat the back of the tracing paper with spray adhesive and stick it to the window. Draw the design you want onto the paper and peel it off the window. Cut out the design, re-apply the spray adhesive, and stick it to the window again. Following the instructions on the can, spray the glass with frosting spray.

GETTING IT RIGHT

The frosting spray will drift in the air, so all areas around the window should be covered and curtains removed before you begin. Gently clean the finished window with a soft cloth because it can be prone to scratching. Further layers of spray can be applied to cover any damage.

3 To subtly obscure areas of clear glass, lightly spray short bursts of frosting onto them.

You can use this technique in conjunction with almost any pattern. If you are not confident about drawing your own design, enlarge a motif on a photocopier to the right size, trace it, and use that as a template.

SOLUTION 2: *Frosted with film*

THIS is a simple, permanent solution that offers complete privacy while allowing the original amount of light into the room. Frosted film gives a better finish than frosting spray over larger areas because the coverage is totally even and it doesn't scratch.

I Spray the glass with enough thinned detergent solution to mist it, but not so much that it drips.

2 Peel the backing off the top section of the film and position it at the top of the glass. Line it up carefully. The solution will allow you to slide the film around a little on the glass, but not very much.

Peel the backing halfway off and gently smooth the film onto the glass, being careful not to move it at the top. Peel the remainder of the backing off and smooth all the film down.

YOU WILL NEED

- ☐ Water spray bottle with thinned detergent solution— I part detergent to I part water
- ☐ Frosting film the size of the glass
- ☐ Squeegee

Nature of problem:
lack of privacy

Extent of solution:
total privacy

Finish:
frosted

Time:
30 minutes

3 Immediately pull the hard edge of a squeegee over the film, working from the middle to the edges, to press all the air out.

GETTING IT RIGHT

You must position the film accurately and work quickly throughout. The wet surface of the window will begin to activate the adhesive on the reverse of the film on contact, so there is little time for repositioning.

Perfect for a small bathroom, this solution offers total privacy without loss of light.

SOLUTION 3: *Simple voile panels*

VOILE panels hung over the windows are versatile because they offer both total and partial screening. They are also easy to make. Because you hang them on hooks at either end, the bottom screw eyes can be hooked over the top hooks to turn the panel into a half-blind.

YOU WILL NEED

- ☐ Voile fabric the width of the window plus 1 inch (2.5 cm) and the length plus 4 inches (10 cm)
- ☐ Scissors
- ☐ Sewing thread
- ☐ Sewing machine
- ☐ 2 lengths of ¼-inch (6-mm) dowel the width of the panels
- ☐ Matte white latex paint
- ☐ 1-inch (2.5-cm) paintbrush
- ☐ 4 hook and eye screw fittings
- ☐ Bradawl
- ☐ Pencil

Nature of problem:
lack of privacy

Extent of solution:
total privacy

Finish:
flat fabric

Time:
2 hours

1 Measure the window and add an overlap of a minimum of ½ inch (12 mm) and no more than 1 inch (2.5 cm) all around plus 1 inch (2.5 cm) for side seams and 4 inches (10 cm) for top and bottom seams. Make the overlap in scale with the width of the window frame. Cut the fabric to size. Press a ¼-inch (6-mm) double hem on each side and machine stitch it. Press under a double 1-inch (2.5-mm) hem at the top and bottom and machine stitch close to the edge to make channels wide enough to accommodate the dowel.

3 Hold the top of the panel to the window, centering it over the glass. Ask a friend to mark the positions of the eyes on the window frame while you hold the panel. Make pilot holes with a bradawl at each marked point and screw in a hook. The easiest way to do this is to screw in the hook a few turns, then put a pencil through it and turn that to screw the hook in fully.

GETTING IT RIGHT

Wash the fabric before use because it may not be preshrunk. If you don't do this you risk shrinking the blinds when you do wash them.

2 Measure the width of the channels and cut the dowels to the same length. Paint the lengths of dowel white and leave to dry. Screw an eye into each end of both dowels. Thread the dowels through the channels so that the eyes protrude on each side of the voile panel.

4 Hook the panel onto the top hooks. Pull the bottom dowel down until the fabric is taut and mark the positions of the bottom eyes. Screw in hooks as before and hook the bottom eyes onto them.

The use of light, white voile provides a softer edge to the window treatment and allows diffused light into the room.

THE PROBLEM: Window treatments on a budget

Having drapes professionally made in the fabric of your choice can be a very expensive exercise, especially if you have a larger home with many windows. Store-bought, premade drapes are usually available in limited colors and sizes, are often made in cheaper fabric, but are still expensive. If you are a confident seamstress, you can make your own drapes, but not everyone possesses the necessary skills. However, there are low-sew and no-sew solutions that allow you to choose your own colors and coordinate the right weight, texture, and style of window treatment with simple, yet stylish tiebacks.

SOLUTION 1: *Rope tiebacks*

COMMERCIALLY available tiebacks are expensive, but it is easy to make your own from natural or dyed rope. Natural-colored rope, available from yacht chandlers, teamed with sisal twine produces a cool, contemporary tieback that will coordinate with most window treatments and fabric colors.

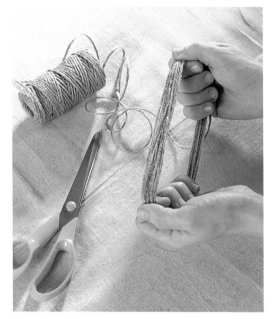

1 Wind the twine around the card approximately 20 times to make an 18-inch (45-cm) long loop. Slip it off the card.

2 Fold the loop in half and place one folded end on two sides of one end of the rope. Bind more twine firmly around the end of the rope, binding over the ends of the loop. Make sure that the binding strands of twine lie smoothly next to one another and completely cover the ends of the loop. Use the point of the scissors to tuck the ends of the binding twine securely under the binding itself.

3 Pinch the loop together at the end of the rope. Bind more twine around the pinch and carry on binding back over the end of the rope, until it meets the previously bound area, then tuck the ends under, as before. Repeat at the other end of the rope.

Fix a hook into the wall at the right point. Take the tieback around the drape and loop the sisal ends over the hook to hold it in place.

YOU WILL NEED

☐ 8-inch (20-cm) wide piece of card

☐ Sisal twine

☐ Scissors

☐ 26-inches (65-cm) thick cotton rope

Nature of problem:
low budget

Extent of solution:
permanent cure

Finish:
rope tiebacks

Time:
30 minutes

> **GETTING IT RIGHT**
>
> *When cutting thick rope, wrap tape tightly around the section to be cut. This stops it from fraying until the ends are bound with the twine.*

Choose rope and twine or fine cord to match your drapes and make completely customized tiebacks.

SOLUTION 2: *Drop cloth drapes*

Dᴿᴼᴾ cloths are generally available in two sizes, 12 x 9 feet (3.5 x 2.8 m) and 12 x 12 feet (3.5 x 3.5 m), and the smaller size is more than sufficient to cover most windows. Drop cloths are made from untreated cotton twill that can either be left natural or dyed in the washing machine. The eyelets you attach to the drop cloths hold the two layers together without any need for sewing. Make certain that they are large enough to slide easily along your curtain rod. Adjust the color of the store-bought dye by using only one packet with each sheet for a faded look or increasing to two or even three packets for a stronger color.

1 Choose two toning dye colors that suit the decorative scheme in your room. Dye the drop cloths in the washing machine,

following the instructions given with the dye. Iron while slightly damp for a smooth finish.

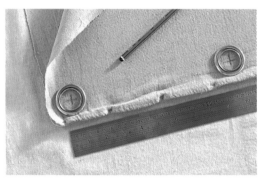

2 Pin the two drop cloths together along the top edge. Lay out the eyelets so that the centers are 1½ inches (3.75 cm) below the top edge with one eyelet at each end and the remainder evenly spaced—approximately every 10 inches (25 cm)—between them. Mark the center of each eyelet position with a pencil cross.

3 Using sharp scissors, cut each cross open through both layers of fabric.

4 Following the instructions given with the eyelets, lay half an eyelet on each side of the fabric, enclosing the cut cross. Position the fixing tool above and below the positioned eyelet and hammer it down until the eyelet is secured in place.

5 Repeat the process until all the eyelets are fastened in place. Most of the fabric around the cross will disappear into the eyelets, but trim off any threads that remain with scissors. Thread the eyelets onto the curtain rod.

Using two different-colored layers not only adds interest but also adds weight to the treatment and helps to cut out light.

YOU WILL NEED

- ☐ Drop cloths
- ☐ Fabric dye
- ☐ Salt
- ☐ Pins
- ☐ 12 1¾-inch (4.5-cm) eyelets
- ☐ Ruler
- ☐ Pencil
- ☐ Scissors
- ☐ Eyelet fixing tool
- ☐ Heavy hammer

Nature of problem:
low budget

Extent of solution:
permanent cure

Finish:
double-layered drape

Time:
1½ hours (after dying)

SOLUTION 3: *Frayed-edge drapes*

A SPEEDY no-sew treatment is a frayed-edge drape hung from café clips. The fold-over at the top not only makes a decorative self-valance, but also gives a thicker, straight edge for the clips to be attached to. This is a good solution for a living room but not appropriate for a bedroom, because the single layer of fabric won't block out all light.

1 Pull out a few threads along the side edge of the fabric until one whole thread pulls out from top to bottom, establishing a straight edge.

2 Using sharp scissors, cut away the loose threads to produce a straight edge.

3 Pull out more whole threads along the same edge until it is frayed to a depth of approximately 1½-inches (4-cm). Repeat the process on all edges of the fabric. Fold over one-fifth of the fabric at the top to make the self-valance. Use café clips to hang the drape from the pole.

YOU WILL NEED

- ☐ Linen or a loose-woven fabric the length of the drop from the curtain rod to the floor, plus one-fifth of that length
- ☐ Scissors
- ☐ Café clips

Nature of problem:
low budget

Extent of solution:
permanent cure

Finish:
self-valance drape

Time:
1 hour

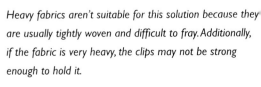

Heavy fabrics aren't suitable for this solution because they are usually tightly woven and difficult to fray. Additionally, if the fabric is very heavy, the clips may not be strong enough to hold it.

SOLUTION 4: *Draped sheer*

THIS low-sew treatment gives stylish results with very little effort. Machine stitch a narrow hem at each cut end of the fabric; leave the selvedge edges as they are. Pull one end of the fabric up behind the curtain pole, pulling it until the other end is just touching the floor. Give it a half-twist and take it back over the pole from the front. Arrange the fabric into two panels with an elegant valance.

This solution looks best on windows that are approximately twice the width of the fabric. Any narrower and you will have to gather the fabric, which spoils the look. If the windows are wider, the fabric won't completely cover them.

YOU WILL NEED

☐ Sheer fabric 2½ times the length of the drop from the curtain pole to the floor

Nature of problem:
low budget

Extent of solution:
permanent cure

Finish:
sheer drape

Time:
30 minutes

SOLUTION 5: *No-sew blanket drapes*

ANOTHER no-sew solution to drapes takes the more unusual approach of using a large blanket as a drape. Because most blankets are relatively small, larger windows are unsuitable for this solution. Loop the blanket over a curtain pole loosely enough to allow it to be easily pulled and adjusted to the right length. Pin through both layers with the kilt pins to hold the blanket in place.

GETTING IT RIGHT

The weight of the chosen blanket shouldn't be too thick, or it will be difficult to pull the drape easily.

The woolen fabric adds a warm and cozy feeling to the room. Because the blanket is thick, this solution is perfect for a bedroom. Any fringing should be arranged so that it appears on the front edge.

YOU WILL NEED

☐ Blanket
☐ Kilt pins

Nature of problem:
low budget

Extent of solution:
permanent cure

Finish:
blanket drape

Time:
20 minutes

SOLUTION 6: *Leather belt tiebacks*

THIS is the simplest solution to tiebacks and requires no effort whatsoever. Choose a belt in a color and style to coordinate with the drapes and the rest of the room. If you don't have a suitable belt, a visit to a thrift store will probably produce one. Fix a hook in the wall at the right height, buckle the belt around the drape and slip the buckle over the hook.

A natural leather belt worked well with this heavy, checked blanket drape, creating a traditional country feel.

YOU WILL NEED

☐ Leather belt

Nature of problem:
low budget

Extent of solution:
permanent cure

Finish:
leather tieback

Time:
10 minutes

ROOMS COME IN many different shapes and sizes, and physically altering the dimensions of a room is an enormous undertaking, involving various professionals and a great deal of money. This chapter aims to solve a wide range of problems by offering alternatives to building work.

Characteristic problems common in many modern homes are narrow or low rooms, while in older properties dark or tall rooms are often an issue. The visual tricks shown in the various solutions not only overcome the problems but also provide a complete decorative scheme for your room, which you can customize by choosing your own colors.

Fireplaces and kitchens are given special mention in this chapter because they both present specific common problems. When older homes are modernized, the mantels and surrounds are often removed and the fireplace boarded up. If you want to use the fireplace again, even just as a recess for a group of lighted candles, you have a potentially expensive problem.

Kitchens are maybe the most costly room to decorate but great results can be achieved for little outlay. The solutions here look at ways of revitalizing kitchen cupboards, the most expensive decorative element of most kitchens.

rooms

THE PROBLEM: **A narrow room**

Available space and badly planned modernization often result in rooms that are very narrow. These spaces can be difficult to work with, but the dimensions can be visually widened using horizontal bands. The result is a deceptively broadened room.

Each of the solutions given here has slightly different benefits beyond this. One forms a soft, central feature wall in the room, making it a good solution for a room that is also plain, while the other helps to reflect light, and adds an extra element of depth to the space.

SOLUTION 1: *Roller stripes*

To use the broadening effect of horizontal stripes but with a more subtle, hand-painted feeling, apply the colors with a small foam roller. Lightly coat the roller with paint, then roll horizontal strokes to create an unstructured series of colored bands without the need for measuring or taping. The deviations from a straight line add to the effect.

YOU WILL NEED

☐ Matte latex paints in complementary colors (see page 23)

☐ Long-pile roller

☐ Roller tray

☐ Foam gloss roller

CORE TECHNIQUES

☐ Painting (see page 24)

Nature of problem:
narrow room

Extent of solution:
visual enhancement

Finish:
uneven stripes

Time:
2 hours

Use the long-pile roller to paint the whole wall with the lightest color as the base. Then add the middle tone, then the darkest colors last of all, with the smaller gloss roller.

GETTING IT RIGHT

If you are unhappy with an aspect of the wall, wait until the paint is dry, then add another band or paint over an existing one. This layering will only serve to increase the visual appeal.

SOLUTION 2: *Mirror tile stripes*

Stick tiles in a single continuous band along all the walls in the room, or in several rows on a feature wall.

THIS is a simple solution that combines the broadening effect of a horizontal band with reflected light. It gives a modern look that would work well in a teenager's bedroom. Draw a line around the room with a spirit level. Stick the adhesive mirror pads to the back of each tile, peel off the backings and stick them onto the wall, using the line as a guide.

Use a small piece of card as a spacer to keep the gaps between the mirror tiles consistent. To maximize the light-reflective qualities, stick the tiles on a wall opposite a window.

YOU WILL NEED

- ☐ Pencil
- ☐ Spirit level
- ☐ Mirror tiles
- ☐ Adhesive mirror pads

Nature of problem:
narrow room

Extent of solution:
visual enhancement

Finish:
mirrored stripes

Time:
I hour

GETTING IT RIGHT

The adhesive pads are very strong, so position the tiles carefully because trying to move them may result in removing the paint from the wall.

THE PROBLEM: **A high-ceilinged room**

High ceilings are generally seen as a positive element in a room, but in a small room they can distort the proportions and make the space feel uncomfortable. These solutions use the same visual principle as narrow rooms—the broadening effect of horizontal bands—in a very specific way. By positioning the bands so that the eye focuses on them, rather than the top of the room, you can lower the visual height of a tall room. Though both solutions use the same principle, they offer totally different looks. In addition, one solution requires only painting, while the other needs basic woodworking skills.

SOLUTION 1: *Wall divided by color*

THIS is a bold solution, not for the faint hearted, and as it will feature as a main component in the room, it should be well planned in complementary tones so as not to overwhelm the space. It is best to use this solution as a feature on the narrowest wall in the room to gain the maximum benefit from the effect while not letting it become too dominant.

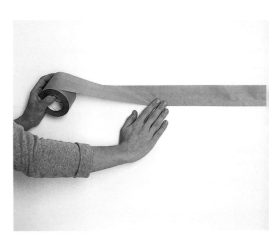

2 Mask off the vertical edges of the wall and the outer edge of each band with painting tape.

3 Using the 2-inch (5-cm) paintbrush, paint each band in the appropriate color and immediately remove the tape. The bands should be in alternate colors, with the highest and lowest bands in the paler color. The widest band, in the middle of the wall, should be in the strong color, so that maximum attention is focused there.

The bold effect is well suited to a kitchen or breakfast room in a modern home.

YOU WILL NEED

- ☐ Matte latex paint in two complementary colors, one pale and one strong, and in white (see page 23)
- ☐ Long-pile roller
- ☐ Roller tray
- ☐ Painting tape
- ☐ Spirit level
- ☐ Pencil
- ☐ 2-inch (5-cm) paintbrush

CORE TECHNIQUES

- ☐ Painting (see page 24)

Nature of problem:
high ceiling

Extent of solution:
visual disguise

Finish:
smooth paint bands

Time:
2 hours

1 Using the long-pile roller, base coat the whole room white or another light color and leave to dry. Using the spirit level and referring to the photograph opposite, mark up the horizontal bands in varying widths with different sized spaces between them. The bands near the top and bottom of the room should be the narrowest, with those in the middle wider.

GETTING IT RIGHT

If paint bleeds under the painting tape it should be left to dry then painted over with the base color. Paint in the bands of the strongest color first, to ensure that the effect isn't too powerful.

SOLUTION 2: *Wall divided with rails*

Mounted on a wide board and waxed for a natural, mellow wood color, the peg rail provides the strong horizontal band needed to visually lower the ceiling and it's balanced by the narrower dado rail. The peg rail should ideally be hung within reach of the smallest person who will use it and approximately 6 inches (15 cm) above the head height of the tallest person. Both rails should run the whole length of the wall.

Measure the wall and buy lumber to suit. The pegs should be spaced approximately every 10 inches (25 cm), and each one is 6 inches (15 cm) long. Using these figures, calculate how much dowel you need to buy.

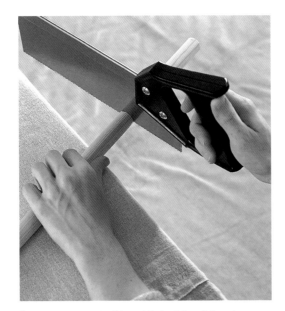

1 Mark the dowel off into 6-inch (15-cm) lengths. Using a backsaw, cut the dowel at the marked points to produce equally sized pieces. Sand the ends smooth.

2 Clamp each length of dowel in a workbench and, using a ⅟₁₆-inch- (1.5-mm-) drill bit, pre-drill a pilot hole in one end.

3 Measure and mark every 10 inches (25 cm) along the wide piece of lumber. Using a ⅛-inch- (3-mm-) drill bit, drill a hole through the lumber at each marked point.

4 Drive a screw into each drilled hole in the lumber so that the end just protrudes. Position the pilot hole in each piece of dowel over the screw. Drive the screw right through the lumber and into the dowel to screw them securely together.

> **GETTING IT RIGHT**
>
> *When cutting the dowel keep the saw as straight as possible. If the end of the dowel isn't straight, it won't sit square on the rail.*

5 Using the 2-inch (5-cm) paintbrush, brush the wax onto the wood quite thickly and evenly.

6 Using the cloth, rub off the excess wax.

Drill holes every 10 inches (25 cm) and use wall plugs or wall board fixings.

YOU WILL NEED

☐ 1-inch- (2.5-cm-) thick dowel

☐ Tape measure

☐ Pencil

☐ Backsaw

☐ Sandpaper

☐ Drill

☐ $\frac{1}{16}$-inch- (1.5-mm-) and $\frac{1}{8}$-inch- (3-mm-) drill bits

☐ ¾ x 6-inch (18-mm x 15-cm) lumber for the peg rail

☐ ¾ x 4-inch (18-mm x 10-cm) lumber for the dado rail

☐ 1½-inch (4-cm) screws (1 for each peg)

☐ Brush-on wax

☐ 2-inch (5-cm) paintbrush

☐ Cloth

Nature of problem:
tall room

Extent of solution:
visual disguise

Finish:
rails

Time:
2 hours

THE PROBLEM: **A low room**

New properties and conversions are particularly prone to this problem. The only solution is to add purely visual height because it's well beyond the scope of the keenest decorator to actually raise the roof.

One of the solutions given concentrates on the wall area, using bold verticals to visually push the ceiling up. The other solution concentrates on the ceiling, giving it a light-reflective finish to make it look higher.

SOLUTION 1: *Painted stripes*

V ERTICAL stripes will make a room look higher, but can also make it narrower. To avoid this, place the stripes only in a central point, such as a chimney breast. The widest stripe should be 4 inches (10 cm) and the narrowest 1 inch (2.5 cm).

Use the method described in *Wall Divided by Color* (see page 140) to paint the stripes.

YOU WILL NEED

☐ Pencil

☐ Spirit level

☐ Painting tape

☐ Matte latex paint in three shades of the same color and in white (see page 23)

☐ 1-inch (2.5-cm) paintbrush

CORE TECHNIQUES

☐ Painting (see page 24)

Nature of problem:
low room

Extent of solution:
visual enhancement

Finish:
painted stripes

Time:
2 hours

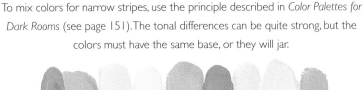

Color palettes for low rooms

To mix colors for narrow stripes, use the principle described in *Color Palettes for Dark Rooms* (see page 151). The tonal differences can be quite strong, but the colors must have the same base, or they will jar.

Shades of fawn are quite neutral and will work well in a small room.

Shades of lilac will soften and warm a room. They are quite intense and are best used in a larger space.

A green palette suits a formal room, whether it be large or small. Always paint the narrowest stripes in the darkest color and the widest ones in the palest color to strengthen the effect.

SOLUTION 2: *Silver ceiling*

THE metallic, light-reflective qualities of silver paint add a different dimension to the ceiling, increasing the feeling of height by making it visually less solid so it loses its sense of proximity and weight. Test the paint beforehand to see how much the brush marks show up. If they show a lot, use the *Mottled Painting* technique (see page 26). If there is no cornice, drop the ceiling to wall join 2 inches (5 cm), but no more, because a deeper band can make the ceiling appear lower.

Measure and mark the wall 2 inches (5 cm) down from the ceiling. Use a spirit level to draw a straight line at the marked point and mask it off. Paint the ceiling and masked-off wall silver. One coat of a good paint should give you a solid finish.

GETTING IT RIGHT

Because silver paint generally has better coverage than average latex, the rule of the order of painting—ceilings, walls, then woodwork—should be changed to walls, ceiling, then woodwork.

The quality of the silver paint is very important. Poorer quality paints are low on metallic pigment and look gray rather than silver.

YOU WILL NEED

- ☐ Pencil
- ☐ Ruler
- ☐ Spirit level
- ☐ Painting tape
- ☐ Silver paint (see page 23)
- ☐ 2-inch (5-cm) paintbrush

CORE TECHNIQUES

- ☐ Painting (see page 24)

Nature of problem:
low room

Extent of solution:
visual enhancement

Finish:
light-reflective

Time:
3 hours

THE PROBLEM: **A small room**

Most homes of any size have at least one small room. Using different colors in that room simply serves to make it appear even smaller. This is because any sectioning up of the room visually reduces the surface area as opposed to maximizing it. Therefore, the best approach is to use one color on either the walls and ceiling or the floor and walls.

There may be a temptation to have all the surfaces the same color, but you run the risk of making the room feel like a little box.

SOLUTION 1: *Walls and ceiling one color*

THIS is a particularly good solution for a small room that also has a low ceiling. The continuation of the same color allows the eye to sweep over it, providing a feeling of greater surface area. Since you are using only one color, play it safe and select a pale tone.

YOU WILL NEED

☐ Matte latex paint (see page 23)

☐ 4-inch (10-cm) paintbrush

CORE TECHNIQUES

☐ Painting (see page 24)

If you are painting textured surfaces as here, use a paintbrush rather than a long-pile roller.

GETTING IT RIGHT

If the walls or ceiling are uneven or damaged, treat them in the same way with the same level of texture. This will further increase the sense of continuity and produce a better overall finish.

Nature of problem: **small room**

Extent of solution: **visual enhancement**

Finish: **painted**

Time: **4 hours**

SOLUTION 2: *Floor and walls one color*

THIS solution is better for a small room with a high ceiling. The floor area looks larger when the floorboards are the same color as the walls. You can paint the ceiling a stronger color, which will make it look lower. If you want to have carpet in the room, simply match a paint color to the chosen carpet to achieve the same effect.

YOU WILL NEED

☐ Matte latex paint (see page 23)

☐ 4-inch (10-cm) paintbrush

☐ Long-pile roller

☐ Roller tray

CORE TECHNIQUES

☐ Painting (see page 24)

Nature of problem:
small room

Extent of solution:
visual enhancement

Finish:
painted

Time:
5 hours

Bare floorboards can look rather hard, so if you want to put rugs down, choose ones that are similar in tone to the floor and don't put them too close to the walls.

GETTING IT RIGHT

Use a roller to paint the walls first. On the floor, follow the preparation and instructions for Tinted with Paint (see page 80), but use a solid color rather than pickling stain. Seal the floor with two coats of floor varnish or polyurethane.

THE PROBLEM: **A dark room**

Natural light is an essential element for any interior space, but all too often outside forces reduce the amount of light a room receives. A number of factors can cause this: the close proximity of other buildings, basement living, overgrown gardens, or just small windows. Painting the room white can make it feel cold, so these solutions allow color to be used without overwhelming the room.

SOLUTION 1: *Mirrored alcoves*

MIRRORS have traditionally been used to add depth to a room because they reflect light. However, a large mirror in a living space can be a little disconcerting, because they reflect your daily life. A more subtle use of mirrors behind shelves makes the most of the light without dominating the room. Glass suppliers will cut mirrors to size— you just stick them in place with special adhesive.

YOU WILL NEED

☐ Pieces of mirror glass cut to the required size and with polished edges

☐ Mirror adhesive

Nature of problem: **dark room**

Extent of solution: **visual enhancement**

Finish: **mirror**

Time: **30 minutes**

Keep the display on the shelf minimal to allow the mirror to reflect the maximum amount of light.

GETTING IT RIGHT

Have the glass cut ¼ inch (6 mm) short of the actual measurements to allow for any discrepancies or surface unevenness in the alcove.

SOLUTION 2: *Walls painted different shades*

IN a room with only one window, use three shades of the same color. Paint the wall with the window in it the darkest shade and the wall opposite it the lightest shade. Paint the two side walls in the mid-tone. This color scheme visually enhances the light coming from the window, and also provides color interest.

Soft, minty greens create a cool feel in a bathroom. Other color palettes may be more suited to rooms with different functions.

Color palettes for dark rooms

To mix colors to exact, graded tones, follow this simple principle. Choose the darkest shade, then add measured amounts of white paint to achieve the lighter shades. For the mid-tone, mix equal quantities of the color and white, and for the lightest tone add two parts white to one part color. Because it's very difficult to match colors exactly, always mix more than you need to avoid running out of a custom-mixed tone.

A bedroom should be a peaceful, tranquil place, associated with rest and relaxation. A soft, warm blue is easy on the eye without being too feminine.

A living room has a slight duality in that it acts as the main reception room, while also being a homey, cozy area. Paler terracotta colors will give a smart feel, but also exude a feeling of warmth.

A kitchen is a lively, dynamic area, lending itself to sunny colors in natural tones. Stone yellow gives a fresh, clean look without being too acidic or over-bearing.

When a wide variety of colors are used in isolation in different rooms, the color in the hall must provide a link between them. A neutral palette of taupe shades provides a good solution for most color schemes and also gives a slightly formal feel, appropriate for a main entrance.

YOU WILL NEED

- ☐ Matte latex paints in three shades of the same color (see page 23)
- ☐ Long-pile roller
- ☐ Roller tray

CORE TECHNIQUES

- ☐ Painting (see page 24)

Nature of problem:
dark room

Extent of solution:
visual enhancement

Finish:
color

Time:
6 hours

SOLUTION 3: *Reflective wall*

A SUBTLE, light-reflective, and highly decorative solution for a dark room is to use silver paint and a pale color in stripes of equal width. The metallic surface will bounce light into other parts of the room, creating a brighter feel. The strength of the wall color should match the tone of the silver, creating equal visual weight between the stripes.

YOU WILL NEED

- ☐ Matte latex paint (see page 23)
- ☐ Silver paint (see page 23)
- ☐ Long-pile roller
- ☐ Roller tray
- ☐ Spirit level
- ☐ Pencil
- ☐ Painting tape
- ☐ 2-inch (5-cm) paintbrush

CORE TECHNIQUES

- ☐ Painting (see page 24)

Nature of problem:
dark room

Extent of solution:
visual enhancement

Finish:
light-reflective stripes

Time:
8 hours

Contemporary and elegant, this solution can be used in most rooms, although positioning a lot of furniture against the walls would lessen the impact of the look.

GETTING IT RIGHT

Use the technique described in Wall Divided by Color (see page 140) to mark out and paint silver stripes over the pale base color. Make all the stripes the same width to avoid visually distorting the dimensions of the room.

THE PROBLEM: **A dark corridor**

A corridor is often completely internal, with no windows, and therefore no natural light. Short of major building work, there is little that can be done to remedy this. These solutions look at making the most of what light is available. One solution makes use of a large mirror to reflect light into the space. This will be less alarming in a corridor than a room, as you don't actually live in the corridor. The other solution channels natural light from another room into the corridor. Both solutions require some knowledge of do-it-yourself techniques, but the results are well worth the work.

SOLUTION I: *Mirrored door*

A wide border of pale green vertical stripes adds interest and visual height to the corridor.

THIS isn't an inexpensive solution, but it does work amazingly well. If the door is reasonably flush to the molding simply have a piece of mirror cut to size. Ask the supplier to polish the edges. Attach the mirror to the door with mirror adhesive. If the door is recessed, have the mirror cut half an inch smaller all the way around to allow the door to swing freely.

YOU WILL NEED

☐ Mirror the size of the door and with polished edges

☐ Mirror adhesive

Nature of problem:
dark córridor

Extent of solution:
viusal enhancement

Finish:
light-reflective door

Time:
I hour

GETTING IT RIGHT

Measure the position of the doorknob exactly and have a hole cut for this at the same time as you have the mirror cut. You will have to take the door off its hinges and lay it flat to attach the mirror. Ask the glass supplier to recommend the right adhesive, because this mirror will be heavy and must be securely fastened to the door.

SOLUTION 2: *Frosted plastic paneled door*

AN alternative approach to resolving dark areas in a corridor is channeling natural light from a room, or rooms, directly off the corridor. Remove the top panels of a door and replace them with frosted plastic. The room will still have a sense of privacy, and the dark corridor will receive natural light. Have your supplier cut the plastic to size.

1 Measure and draw a line ¼ inch (6 mm) inside the edge of the panels in the top of the door. Drill a hole in each corner, just inside the pencil line.

2 Slip the blade of the jigsaw into a drilled hole and saw along the pencil line to the next hole. Repeat on each edge until you have cut the entire panel out of the door.

YOU WILL NEED

- ☐ Pencil
- ☐ Ruler
- ☐ Drill
- ☐ ½-inch (12-mm) drill bit
- ☐ Jigsaw
- ☐ 120-grit sandpaper
- ☐ Sanding block
- ☐ Clear sealant
- ☐ Frosted plastic panels the size of the top door panels

Nature of problem:
dark corridor

Extent of solution:
physical enhancement

Finish:
light panels

Time:
2 hours

3 Sand the cut edges smooth.

4 Squeeze a line of clear sealant along the ¼-inch (6-mm) lip around each panel and place the frosted plastic panel on top of it. Wipe away any excess sealant and leave to dry.

GETTING IT RIGHT

The finish on either side of the door will be different, as one side has a lumber lip and the other doesn't. If this concerns you, cut lengths of beading to size, mitering the corners for a neat fit, and stick them over the visible edges of the plastic with contact adhesive.

One or more of the doors leading into the corridor can be treated in this way to completely change the nature of the space.

THE PROBLEM: A "junction" room

A junction room—where many rooms lead off from one area—is most common in hallways and on landings, but is also a problem in walk-through rooms that connect different parts of the house and bedrooms with ensuite bathrooms. Multiple doors have a tendency to make the space feel congested, and the white molding around each door breaks into the wall color, fragmenting the space and making it feel smaller. There are two simple ways to solve this problem. The first solution directly incorporates the doors into the decorative scheme and the second breaks from the traditional concept of painting the woodwork in a different color than the wall.

SOLUTION 1: *Painted bands*

A REALLY adventurous solution is to paint bold stripes directly across all the doors. The eye is drawn to the bands of color and the doors seem to almost completely vanish. Use the method described in *Wall Divided by Color* (see page 140) to paint stripes on the walls and doors. Use the 1-inch (2.5-cm) paintbrush to hand-paint the line across the molding. You can touch up any mistakes once the paint is dry.

For simplicity and impact each band is exactly the same width. Measure the height of the room and divide it by seven. Don't be tempted to make the stripes narrower than this or the result could be visual chaos.

YOU WILL NEED

- ☐ Matte latex paint in two colors (see page 23)
- ☐ Long-pile roller
- ☐ Roller tray
- ☐ Spirit level
- ☐ Pencil
- ☐ Ruler
- ☐ Painting tape
- ☐ 2-inch (5-cm) paintbrush
- ☐ 1-inch (2.5-cm) square-ended, flat paintbrush

CORE TECHNIQUES

- ☐ Painting (see page 24)

Nature of problem:
no detail

Extent of solution:
visual disguise

Finish:
painted bands

Time:
5 hours

Color palettes for junction rooms

The color of the highest band will either visually raise or lower the ceiling; paint a dark band at the top to lower the ceiling or a light one to raise it. Remember, the more contrasting the colors of the stripes are, the stronger the final effect will be. The bold charcoal and off-white used right, works well in this modern office but wouldn't be very comfortable in a bedroom.

Lighter tones of mid-blue and palest blue make the overall effect softer.

Complementary shades of terra-cotta and pale beige will add warmth without the strips becoming too strong.

SOLUTION 2: *Painted one color*

EMPHASIS can be diverted from the doors by using the same color over the walls, doors, molding, and baseboards. This gives an overall color continuity and a sense of enlargement. Paint the woodwork with the paintbrush using eggshell paint mixed to exactly match the roller-painted walls.

YOU WILL NEED

☐ Matte latex paint (see page 23)

☐ Matching eggshell paint (see page 23)

☐ Long-pile roller

☐ Roller tray

☐ 2-inch (5-cm) paintbrush

CORE TECHNIQUES

☐ Painting (see page 24)

Nature of problem:
junction room

Extent of solution:
visual disguise

Finish:
color

Time:
5 hours

As with small rooms, only one color can be chosen, so play it safe and use a fairly pale tone.

GETTING IT RIGHT

The sheen level of eggshell paint is closest to that of matte latex and helps to keep the doors at the same visual level as the walls.

THE PROBLEM: A plain room with no architectural detail

Architectural detail is generally associated with older properties. The greater the age, the more detailing such as fireplaces, alcoves, cornices, ceiling roses, feature windows, deep moldings, and baseboards. But because these serve a purely decorative purpose, most modern properties have few, if any, of these elements. If there is existing architectural detail, the decorative scheme can be very plain, but if a room is devoid of any features at all, the scheme becomes very important because it's the only source of decoration. The solution is to create an interesting focal point in a plain room, usually a feature wall.

SOLUTION 1: *Papered feature panel*

GETTING IT RIGHT

Don't use two patterned papers together because they may fight. Choose a patterned paper and a plain one that picks out a color in the pattern.

THIS is a simple solution that relies on the pattern of the paper to provide a decorative focal point. Any sort of paper can be used: handmade textures, gift wrap, borders, or wallpapers. Structured patterns with a small repeat, plain colors, and metallic finishes are the easiest to divide up and arrange and can be teamed together to provide bold contrasts.

Plan the arrangement and cut pieces of paper to size. Draw a vertical line on the wall as a positioning guide. Use the traditional wallpapering technique to attach each piece to the wall.

Vary the size of the panel according to the proportions of the room. Plan the arrangement to accentuate the pattern on the chosen paper.

YOU WILL NEED

☐ Paper
☐ Pencil
☐ Ruler
☐ Craft knife
☐ Cutting mat
☐ Wallpaper paste
☐ Pasting paintbrush
☐ Papering brush

CORE TECHNIQUES

☐ Painting (see page 24)

Nature of problem:
no detail

Extent of solution:
visual enhancement

Finish:
papered panel

Time:
I hour

SOLUTION 2: *Projection-painted feature wall*

THE most visually striking of the solutions, this is an ideal way to decorate a large plain wall and is a lot easier to achieve than it appears. An image can be adjusted to fit any sized wall by altering the position of the projector. However, this technique isn't suitable for small rooms because you may not be able to get the projector far enough away from the wall. Decide on the image you want, trace it onto acetate, and then rent a projector.

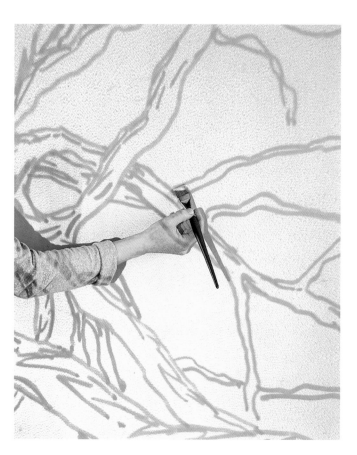

YOU WILL NEED

☐ Image

☐ Acetate film

☐ Fine permanent pen

☐ Overhead projector

☐ Matte latex paint
   (see page 23)

☐ 1-inch (2.5-cm)
   square-ended, flat
   paintbrush

Nature of problem:
no detail

Extent of solution:
visual enhancement

Finish:
painted picture

Time:
4 hours

1 Paint the wall in a solid background color. Lay a sheet of acetate film over the image and trace it with the pen. Lay the acetate on top of the projector and adjust it until you are happy with the position of the projected image on the wall. Dip the paintbrush into a lighter shade of the background color and using light side-to-side strokes, sketch over the projected lines.

2 Once you have sketched the outline of the image, turn off the projector. Fill in the image using more sketchy brush-strokes to make sure that the picture doesn't become too solid.

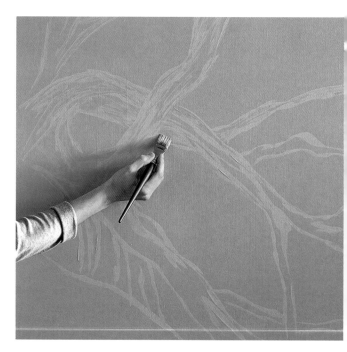

The image is traced, and the size of the finished piece will have such an impact that the quality of the paint work isn't important. Therefore you don't have to be artistic to attempt this solution.

SOLUTION 3: *Painted picture border*

IF there is a great expanse of wall and a picture is dwarfed in proportion to it, a border can visually increase the size of the piece, drawing emphasis toward it and away from the wall. This is a good solution for pictures without frames because the border gives the picture a definite edge.

1 Using a pencil, draw around the picture. Take it off the wall. Measure and draw further borders 2 inches (5 cm) and 4 inches (10 cm) from the original line.

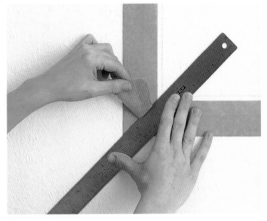

2 Mask off the inside edge of the outer border with painting tape. To miter the corners, tape along the line, extending the tape about 2 inches (5 cm) beyond each end. Place a ruler at 45 degrees across the tape, and carefully tear the tape along it. Repeat the process at both ends, ensuring that the corners make a perfect 90 degrees.

3 Dip the tip of the paintbrush into the paint, wipe off the excess until it's almost dry, and brush along the tape, stroking up and down to create a soft shadow without any hard edges. Peel off the tape.

YOU WILL NEED

☐ Pencil

☐ Ruler

☐ Painting tape

☐ Matte latex paint (see page 23)

☐ 2-inch (5-cm) paintbrush

CORE TECHNIQUES

☐ Painting (see page 24)

Nature of problem:
no detail

Extent of solution:
visual enhancement

Finish:
painted border

Time:
1 hour

4 Mask just inside the inner line in the same way as in Step 2. Dry-brush along the tape in the same way as in Step 3. Peel off the tape and leave to dry before re-hanging the picture.

GETTING IT RIGHT

Once the brush has been loaded with paint, start painting lightly until most of the paint has been evenly brushed on, then apply more pressure as the brush becomes drier.

A textured wall is ideal for this solution, as the texture will help to keep the painted border soft, with only the raised areas picking up paint. On smooth walls you need to be more careful, keeping the brush dry and building up layers until a soft, even border is achieved.

THE PROBLEM: **A plain fireplace**

Fireplaces are usually found in older homes, and all too often the mantel and surround are no longer present. This is because they have been removed as a valuable commodity (there is a booming trade in secondhand fireplaces), or because the house was unsympathetically modernized and the traditional features were deemed unsuitable for the new scheme. The end result is an ugly hole in the wall or a grate with no surround. You could, of course, just have the fireplace blocked up (hire a professional to do this to avoid ventilation problems).

Alternatively you can use these solutions to make the fireplace a decorative feature once again. Even if the chimney isn't in working order (you must get this checked before lighting a fire), the fireplace can be used to hold candles or flowers.

SOLUTION 1: *Traditional faux fire surround*

MAKE a frame from 8-inch (20-cm) wide MDF, screw a shelf along the top and fix to the wall with project glue. Paint the surround with satin paint and seal it with two coats of heat-resistant varnish.

YOU WILL NEED

☐ MDF cut to size

☐ Drill

☐ Drill bit

☐ Screws

☐ Project glue

☐ 2-inch (5-cm) paintbrush

☐ Satin paint

☐ White spirit

☐ Primer/Undercoat

☐ Clear heat-resistant varnish

CORE TECHNIQUES

☐ Painting (see page 24)

Nature of problem:
plain fireplace

Extent of solution:
permanent cure

Finish:
faux fire surround

Time:
4 hours

For a subtle paint effect, brush a little paint thinner over the satin panel while it is still wet. Colorwash the wall around the fireplace to complement the paint effect on the new surround.

GETTING IT RIGHT

If the surround isn't flush to the wall, fill down the sides and along the top, then paint the filler. This will make the surround look more solid with a neater finish.

SOLUTION 2: *Gilded cover*

THIS solution is for a fireplace that isn't in use. The opening is covered and the central hole ventilates the chimney and offers a display point. The board must be flush to the wall, so measure the fireplace and, if necessary, cut the baseboards back. Fix the board to the wall with project glue.

YOU WILL NEED

- ☐ Square of ¼-inch (6-mm) MDF, 2 inches (5 cm) taller and wider than the fireplace
- ☐ Tape measure
- ☐ Pencil
- ☐ Drill
- ☐ ¼-inch (6-mm) drill bit
- ☐ Jigsaw
- ☐ 120-grit sandpaper
- ☐ Light gold paint
- ☐ 2-inch (5-cm) paintbrush
- ☐ Small sponge roller
- ☐ Japan gold size
- ☐ Copper transfer leaf
- ☐ Soft brush
- ☐ Gloss spray varnish
- ☐ Project glue

CORE TECHNIQUES

- ☐ Painting (see page 24)

Nature of problem:
plain fireplace

Extent of solution:
permanent

Finish:
decorative cover

Time:
3 hours

I Mark out a circle on the MDF. This design is a 12 inch (30 cm) diameter circle positioned centrally across a 33 inch- (84 cm-) square panel, 8 inches (20 cm) up from the bottom. Drill a hole just inside the circle, slot the blade of the jigsaw into the hole and carefully cut around the marked circle. Sand the edges smooth.

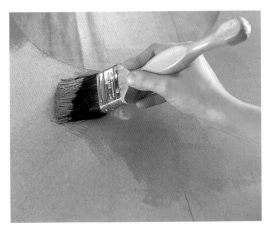

2 Using the 2-inch (5-cm) paintbrush, brush gold paint onto the board and then use a side-to-side motion to create a crosshatched effect in the paint. Leave to dry.

4 Lay a sheet of transfer leaf over a section of stamped circles and press it down. Rub the back with a soft brush to ensure that the leaf adheres well to the size. Peel off the backing, and any leaf sticking to it. Repeat until you have covered the whole board. Brush off any loose flecks of copper leaf with a soft brush and seal the board with gloss spray varnish.

> ### GETTING IT RIGHT
> *Peel the backing of the transfer leaf away slowly, bit by bit, and if a lot of leaf is still attached, place it back down in the same position and continue to rub until it adheres to the surface. Don't worry too much if the finish is a little patchy—this just adds to the effect.*

3 Dip the end of the mini roller into the gold size and stamp circles onto the paint. Position the first circle at top center of the board, and stamp out on each side towards the edge, butting each circle up to the last one. The size becomes tacky in about half an hour, so you have enough time to stamp half of the board before staring to apply the copper leaf.

Paint the walls, or even just the chimney breast, a strong color to complement the rich, metallic colors of the fireplace cover.

SOLUTION 3: *Wooden surround*

If the hearth is also missing, consider using large paving slabs because they fit in well with the rustic quality of the wooden surround.

THIS solution is suited to larger "holes" with rough brick edges. Measure and mount the frame so that the inner edge overlaps the edge of the hole by at least several inches (cm), this ensures that the rough edges are covered. Miter the corner joins then fix the frame in place with project glue to avoid screw holes.

YOU WILL NEED

☐ 2 pieces of lumber the height of the fireplace, mitered at the top.

☐ 1 piece of lumber the width of the fireplace, mitered at each end.

☐ Saw

☐ Miter block

☐ Project glue

Nature of problem:
plain fireplace

Extent of solution:
permanent

Finish:
fire surround

Time:
1 hour

GETTING IT RIGHT

The wood will need to be treated to seal and protect it using wax, paint, pickling stain, varnish or stain. If left unsealed the lumber will mark easily and permanently.

SOLUTION 4: *Painted surround*

IF the grate is still present but the surround has been removed, a simple and inexpensive solution is to paint a border around the grate. This should be approximately the same size as the original surround, so find a picture of a similar grate to the one you have and copy the proportions. Measure and mark out the border and mask it off with painting tape. Paint the border and immediately peel off the tape.

YOU WILL NEED

☐ Pencil

☐ Ruler

☐ Painting tape

☐ Matte latex paint

☐ 2-inch (5-cm) paintbrush

CORE TECHNIQUES

☐ Painting (see page 24)

Nature of problem:
plain fireplace

Extent of solution:
visual enhancement

Finish:
painted surround

Time:
30 minutes

A bracketless shelf fixed along the top edge of the border, and painted in the same color, will cover the top of the grate.

GETTING IT RIGHT

If the fireplace itself is shabby, but it's still in use, smarten it up by painting it with a heat-resistant paint, available from fireplace suppliers.

THE PROBLEM: **Uncoordinated soft furnishings**

Coordinating soft furnishings into a room scheme can be tricky. If you have a mixture of patterns or colors in a room, the result can look untidy. It is usually best to simplify the soft furnishing elements such as cushions and curtains as far as possible. The solutions here look at tying a fabric into an interior scheme through repeated pattern and uniting different soft furnishings while keeping them interesting.

SOLUTION 1: *Remnant cushions*

To avoid a patchwork look, use the drape fabric and the remnant fabric in equal quantities on each cushion front.

HAVING all the soft furnishings in a room in the same pattern makes for a very formal look. A more relaxed style can be achieved by using one fabric for the largest pieces, usually the drapes, and matching that with other fabrics for smaller soft furnishings. Here, remnants in the same colors, but different patterns, have been teamed with leftover drape fabric to make cushions.

YOU WILL NEED

- ☐ Fabrics
- ☐ Scissors
- ☐ Sewing machine
- ☐ Sewing thread
- ☐ Cushion pad or filling

Nature of problem:
soft furnishings

Extent of solution:
permanent cure

Finish:
patterned cushions

Time:
1 hour

SOLUTION 2: *Stamped walls*

IF the drapes are patterned and the walls plain, the drapes can look isolated in the room. Reproduce a motif in the fabric as a stamp, and stamp a border or all-over wallpaper pattern on the wall to unite the two elements.

1 Lay the fabric out flat and place a piece of tracing paper over the area of pattern you want to reproduce. Using the pencil, trace over the pattern.

2 Spray the glue onto the back of the tracing paper and stick it onto the foam rubber. Using a sharp craft knife, cut around the outline of the motif on the tracing paper, and through the foam rubber. Pull away the excess foam rubber to make the outer edge of the stamp.

3 Working carefully, cut along the traced lines within the stamp, cutting through the paper and approximately ¼ inch (6 mm) into the foam rubber. Be sure not to cut right through the rubber. Remove the tracing paper.

YOU WILL NEED

- ☐ Patterned fabric
- ☐ Tracing paper
- ☐ Pencil
- ☐ Spray glue
- ☐ 1-inch (2.5-cm) thick high-density foam rubber
- ☐ Craft knife
- ☐ Gloss roller
- ☐ Roller tray
- ☐ Matte latex paint
- ☐ Medium artist's paintbrush

Nature of problem:
soft furnishings

Extent of solution:
permanent cure

Finish:
stamped walls

Time:
2 hours

4 Pinch a section of foam between cut lines, and carefully cut underneath it with the craft knife. Lift it further and cut again until you have cut out the whole section. Repeat until you have cut out the whole design.

5 Use a gloss roller to coat the stamp with paint. Ensure that all the raised surfaces are covered, but don't apply the paint too thickly.

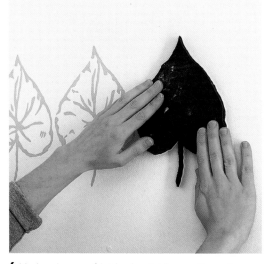

However well the stamp is made or applied, don't try to reproduce the fabric design in the same color. It is very unlikely that you will be able to create a perfect match, so it's best that it looks intentionally different. To achieve this, simply reverse the color, matching the paint to the main fabric color.

6 Having drawn a faint horizontal line on the wall as a positional guide, press the stamp onto the wall, ensuring that the entire painted surface makes contact with the wall. Lift the stamp off cleanly. Leave to dry.

7 Dilute a little of the same color with a little water (1 part paint to 1 part water), then brush over the design to fill it in. Make sure that you don't paint outside the edge of the stamp.

THE PROBLEM: Old wooden cupboard doors

The fastest way to update a kitchen is to replace the cupboard doors. However, this is an expensive option, particularly if at some point in the future you want to replace the entire kitchen and are looking for a stopgap until then. Fortunately, there is a range of solutions for making the most of old or damaged kitchen cupboard doors at low cost. Wooden doors are the most versatile, because they can be easily cut, painted, and added to.

The importance of the cupboard door handles can't be underestimated, and they are definitely worth spending money on. The plainer the doors are, the more decorative or larger the handles should be. If the new handles will be in a different position than the old ones, fill the old holes before you start.

Before you treat them, clean and sand all wooden doors to remove grease and provide a well-keyed surface to paint over.

SOLUTION 1: Tongue-and-groove paint effect

THOUGH this effect appears complex, it's very simple to achieve. But it does take a little time. The original wood acts as the base color, and the grain remains visible to add realism. The trick, as with any effect that imitates a real surface, is to plan the arrangement carefully. For this effect, the width of the planks should be about 4 inches (10 cm), though ½ inch (12 mm) either way is acceptable.

1 Measure and mark out the planks on the door. If you can't make all of them an equal width, ensure that the two outside ones, though a different width than the inner planks, are the same.

2 Stick a length of masking tape over each pencil line, pressing it down firmly.

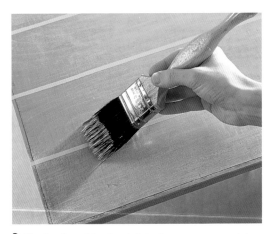

3 Dip the tips of the brush into the warm gray paint and dry-brush a light coat over the whole door. Use long strokes and follow the direction of the grain in the wood. Immediately peel off the masking tape. Leave to dry for approximately 1 hour.

4 Using the beige paint, dry-brush lightly over the whole door again. This should be a very thin coat of paint, so that the original color and the groove lines are not obscured. Leave to dry overnight before hanging the door.

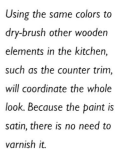

Using the same colors to dry-brush other wooden elements in the kitchen, such as the counter trim, will coordinate the whole look. Because the paint is satin, there is no need to varnish it.

GETTING IT RIGHT

- *If you apply the top coat too thickly and the groove lines disappear, use a dry cloth to immediately wipe off the excess paint.*
- *As the wood grain is still visible, it's better to use the original handle holes with this solution.*

5 Dry-brush a wooden doorknob in the same colors to match it to the door.

YOU WILL NEED

- ☐ Pencil
- ☐ Ruler
- ☐ ¼-inch (6-mm) masking tape
- ☐ Satin paint in warm gray and pale beige (see page 23)
- ☐ 2-inch (5-cm) paintbrush

CORE TECHNIQUES

- ☐ Painting (see page 24)

Nature of problem:
old doors

Extent of solution:
visual enhancement

Finish:
faux wood

Time:
1½ hours

SOLUTION 2: *Added wooden beading*

Bᴇᴄᴀᴜsᴇ the original surface is completely covered and any existing damage can be filled and repaired, this is the perfect solution for doors that are in particularly bad condition. There are many widths and different profiles of molding available, but to keep the look crisp, it's best to choose something simple.

1 Kitchen cupboard doors come in standard sizes and the measurements given are for a 19½ x 28-inch (50 x 70-cm) door. Measure and mark a 4-inch (10-cm) border around the door. Within the central area, measure and mark five equally spaced vertical lines.

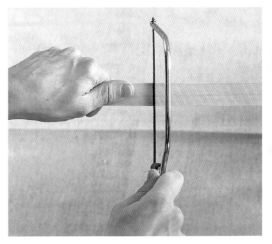

2 Cut five lengths of molding to fit the marked lines. Sand the cut ends smooth, but don't round the corners.

3 Run a line of wood glue along the back of each length of molding, and lay it over a marked line. Press the molding down, and immediately wipe away any excess glue with the damp cloth. Leave to dry.

4 Prime the door, making sure that the brushstrokes are laid off in long strokes to keep the painted surface as flat and smooth as possible. Leave to dry. Paint the wood using the paintbrush and the satin paint. To achieve a really smooth painted finish, very lightly sand the whole surface between each coat. Apply a good amount of paint, so the brushstrokes can be smoothed out, but not so much that the paint starts to pool and drip.

Decorate the drawer fronts with horizontal strips of molding to match them to the doors.

YOU WILL NEED

☐ Pencil
☐ Ruler
☐ Wooden molding
☐ Small saw
☐ 120-grit sandpaper
☐ Strong wood adhesive
☐ Damp cloth
☐ Primer undercoat (see page 23)
☐ 2-inch (5-cm) paintbrush
☐ Satin paint (see page 23)

CORE TECHNIQUES

☐ Painting (see page 24)

Nature of problem: **old doors**

Extent of solution: **physical enhancement**

Finish: **ridged surface**

Time: **I hour**

GETTING IT RIGHT

If you have different-sized doors in your kitchen, keep the border measurement the same and the spacing between the lengths of molding on the different doors reasonably consistent. It is fine to have different numbers of moldings on different doors, but the spacing must be the same.

SOLUTION 3: Metal gauze panels

INSTEAD of adding material to the doors, this solution initially involves taking existing material away. Wooden doors can be easily cut, or new medium density fiberboard panels can be cut to size. Use the technique described in *Frosted Plastic Paneled Door* (see page 154) to cut the hole. The primer will take the wax well, whereas satin or eggshell paint would just keep it on the surface.

YOU WILL NEED

- ☐ Door with a central hole
- ☐ Primer (see page 23)
- ☐ 2-inch (5-cm) paintbrush
- ☐ Tinted brush-on wax (page 23)
- ☐ Soft cloth
- ☐ Metal gauze the size of the central hole plus 1 inch (2.5 cm) all round
- ☐ Heavy-duty stapler
- ☐ Staples

CORE TECHNIQUES

- ☐ Painting (see page 24)

Nature of problem:
old doors

Extent of solution:
physical enhancement

Finish:
metal gauze panels

Time:
1 hour

1 Using the paintbrush, prime the whole door, including the inner and outer edges. A solid finish is required, so apply at least two coats. Leave to dry.

3 Immediately buff over the wax with the soft cloth, until all the brush marks have been removed and the effect is even.

2 Brush wax over the surface of the door and along the edges, spreading it evenly over the surface

4 Lay the door face down and position the sheet of metal gauze centrally over the hole. Staple the gauze to the wood all the way around, keeping the tension quite taut.

The country-style look of these cupboards is well suited to a kitchen in an older home.

THE PROBLEM: Old melamine cupboard doors

Melamine is practical and relatively inexpensive and is used extensively in kitchens, especially as cupboard doors. However, after a few years it can look shabby and stained. Replacing all the doors is expensive, so these solutions offer different ways of revitalizing them at little cost.

As with wooden doors, the importance of handles can't be underestimated. They will enhance whatever door treatment you choose and you can remove them and use them in a new kitchen at a later date.

The essential medium needed to paint all melamine is a specialist melamine primer that is formulated to adhere to the surface and act as the perfect undercoat for paint. Don't be tempted to use ordinary wood primer—it won't work.

Rather than unscrewing the hinge from the cupboard door, it's easier to take out the retaining screw in the hinge, separating the hinge into two pieces. When you have finished decorating the door, just re-assemble the hinge.

SOLUTION 1: *Plain paint*

Because the finish is so flat, this is a good solution for doors that are only marked. To achieve a smooth finish, apply the paint with a gloss roller.

1 Lightly sand the whole door to provide a good surface for the primer, then clean the door to remove any dirt or grease. Using the gloss roller, apply the primer in a good, even coat. Leave to dry.

2 Paint the door with the top coat paint, again using the gloss roller to get a smooth surface. Leave to dry overnight and add a second coat if necessary before re-hanging the door.

YOU WILL NEED

- ☐ 120-grit sandpaper
- ☐ Melamine primer (see page 23)
- ☐ Gloss roller
- ☐ Roller tray
- ☐ Satin or eggshell paint (see page 23)

CORE TECHNIQUES

- ☐ Painting (see page 24)

Nature of problem:
old doors

Extent of solution:
visual enhancement

Finish:
smooth paint

Time:
30 minutes

GETTING IT RIGHT

Never stop painting halfway across a door; the edge of the paint will dry and will always show on the finished door.

Choose a paint color to complement other elements in the kitchen. If the color is strong, consider painting the visible areas of the cupboard bodies to match.

SOLUTION 2: *Metal panels*

Metal strips around the edges will cover chipped corners and metal panels will cover larger areas of damage or stain. Choose which to use depending on the condition of each cupboard, as the two can be mixed and matched within the kitchen.

T HIS solution works best on doors that aren't too badly marked or stained. The metal trim can be positioned to cover bad areas, and if necessary, you can paint the door first (page 176). Plan the positioning of the panels straight onto the door, and have metal cut to size by your supplier. If the metal runs over the holes for handles, have these drilled at the same time. Then simply apply contact adhesive to the reverse of each panel and press into position.

YOU WILL NEED

☐ Ruler

☐ Pencil

☐ Metal panels cut to size

☐ Contact adhesive

Nature of problem:
old doors

Extent of solution:
physical enhancement

Finish:
metal bands

Time:
30 minutes

GETTING IT RIGHT

If the panels are large, you can use lengths of masking tape to hold them in position while the glue dries.

SOLUTION 3: *Vinyl covering*

Quick and simple, this solution will also cover a lot of damage with no need for filling or painting. Self-adhesive vinyl is available in a wide range of colors and patterns, including natural materials, such as wood and marble.

Make sure that the door is completely clean before you start so that the vinyl sticks to the surface well.

YOU WILL NEED

☐ Steel ruler
☐ Craft knife
☐ Cutting mat
☐ Self-adhesive vinyl
☐ Dry cloth

Nature of problem:
old doors

Extent of solution:
visual enhancement

Finish:
smooth vinyl

Time:
30 minutes

1 Using a steel ruler and a craft knife, cut a strip of vinyl the width and length of the top edge of the door. Stick the strip across the edge, pulling off the backing paper as you go. Repeat on the bottom edge of the door.

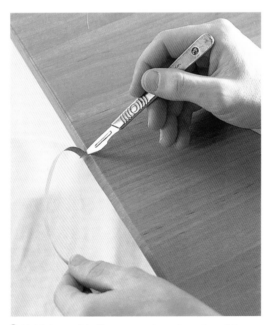

3 Hold the craft knife at an angle to the edge of the door and run it across, cutting away the excess vinyl at the bottom.

> **GETTING IT RIGHT**
>
> *Sticking down the large piece of vinyl to the front of the door can be tricky, so get a friend to help you. One of you slowly pulls the backing paper off and the other smooths the vinyl down.*

2 Cut another piece of vinyl the length of the door plus 1 inch (2.5 cm), by the width plus 2 inches (5 cm). Make sure that one end of the vinyl is exactly straight and at right angles to the sides. Peel 4 inches (10 cm) of the backing away from the straight end, and lay it centrally across the top of the door, aligning the vinyl and door edge carefully. Slowly pull the backing sheet off, smoothing the vinyl down with a cloth as you go. Smooth the excess vinyl at the sides over the edges, to the back of the door.

Turn a shabby, dated kitchen into a stylish modern one by using beech-patterned vinyl to cover the cupboard doors.

SOLUTION 4: *Sprayed doors*

FLECK-stone spray paint creates an instant paint effect, straight from the can. The finish will cover marks and obscure small chips, but deep dents should be filled and sanded first. The base coat should be a darker tone, but the same overall color as the fleck stone. By tinting the primer with a colorizer, you can prime and base coat the door in one go.

1 Tint the primer to a dark gray with black colorizer. Using a gloss roller, apply the tinted primer to the door, ensuring that you cover all the edges. Leave to dry.

2 Following the instructions on the can, spray the door with an even coat of the spray paint. Leave to dry and using the paintbrush, seal with varnish.

YOU WILL NEED

- ☐ Melamine primer
- ☐ Black colorizer
- ☐ Gloss roller
- ☐ Fleck-stone spray paint
- ☐ Varnish
- ☐ 2-inch (5-cm) paintbrush

CORE TECHNIQUES

- ☐ Painting (see page 24)

Nature of problem:
old doors

Extent of solution:
visual enhancement

Finish:
granite effect

Time:
20 minutes

The lightly textured granite effect can be sealed with either a matte varnish for a natural look or high gloss varnish for a polished finish.

GETTING IT RIGHT
Always spray in a well-ventilated area, covering a large area of the floor with drop cloths because the spray drifts.

THE PROBLEM: Missing cupboard doors

If some cupboard doors in a kitchen are missing and you can't match them, there are options beyond buying new doors for all the cupboards. You can either make the open shelves look more attractive or screen them off with fabric. These are quick solutions to the problem and can be used in conjunction with each other or they can be coordinated with any remaining cupboard doors.

SOLUTION 1: *Denim panels*

1 Press under and machine stitch a double 1-inch (2.5-cm) hem down each side of the denim. Repeat at the top and bottom of the panel. Lay a ruler across the top of the panel and mark where the eyelets will go, with one at each end and others spaced evenly between them, approximately every 4 inches (10 cm).

2 Following the instructions on the eyelet kit, insert an eyelet at each marked point.

3 If the cupboard unit has a wooden reveal where the door used to be, you can screw the hooks into that. If not, cut a batten to size, screw the hooks into that and then screw the batten inside the door frame of the unit. To establish the correct position of the hooks, lay the eyelet edge of the denim along the door frame, or over the batten, and mark through the centers of the eyelets onto the wood. Screw in a hook at each marked point.

THESE panels offer instant screening, with easy access by either pulling the fabric aside, or unhooking a few eyelets. Because the panels are flat, only the minimal amount of material is necessary, keeping costs down. If denim doesn't suit your color scheme, any fairly heavy, washable fabric can be used.

YOU WILL NEED

- ☐ Piece of denim the size of the cupboard front plus 2 inches (5 cm) all the way around
- ☐ Sewing machine
- ☐ Sewing thread
- ☐ Ruler
- ☐ Pencil
- ☐ Eyelet kit
- ☐ L-shaped hooks
- ☐ Batten (if required)

Nature of problem:
missing doors

Extent of solution:
physical enhancement

Finish:
fabric panels

Time:
1 hour

Denim is hard-wearing and practical, both in color and durability, and perfectly suited to a kitchen area.

SOLUTION 2: *Wicker baskets*

IF the shelving area is to remain in full view, make it an attractive feature in itself by filling it with wicker baskets. Their use is limited to shelves, so for larger cupboard areas you may want to coordinate them with a fabric screening solution. This solution requires the units to be in good condition because large areas of them are visible and depending on the baskets you buy, it isn't necessarily an inexpensive option.

YOU WILL NEED

☐ Baskets

Nature of problem:
missing doors

Extent of solution:
physical enhancement

Finish:
baskets

Time:
10 minutes

Baskets not only provide effective storage, but also evoke a traditional look that works well in a country-style kitchen.

GETTING IT RIGHT

Measure the width of the shelves and buy baskets to suit. Different sized baskets on different shelves will make the effect less regimented.

SOLUTION 3: *Simple curtains*

Press under and machine sew a double ½-inch (12-mm) hem along the short sides of the fabric. Repeat along the top and bottom edges, but with a double 1-inch (2.5-cm) hem. Following the manufacturer's instructions, cut the curtain wire several inches short of the required length, pull taut, and thread through the hem at the top of the curtain. Screw small hooks into each side of the cupboard and hook the wire onto them to hang the curtain.

SIMPLE gathered curtains offer another fabric screening solution with a softer feel than the panels. They are much easier to make. Hold them on a length of curtain wire hooked underneath the work surface. The style and color of the fabric should be chosen to suit the room, but when starting from scratch, match the wall paint to the fabric because paint is available in a far wider range of colors than fabric is.

YOU WILL NEED

☐ Piece of fabric the length of the cupboard front plus 4 inches (10 cm) and 1½ times the width

☐ Sewing machine

☐ Sewing thread

☐ Curtain wire the width of the cupboard

☐ Small hooks

Nature of problem:
missing doors

Extent of solution:
physical enhancement

Finish:
curtains

Time:
30 minutes

If the curtains are a permanent solution rather than a stopgap until you replace the entire kitchen, consider making curtains to match for the windows.

GETTING IT RIGHT

If covering a wide expanse, make the curtains in sections on the same wire to make access to the shelving easier.

GLOSSARY

Backsaw: a small wood saw.

Base coat: the first coat of paint on a wall, or the color of the paint underneath a paint effect.

Blackboard paint: a paint that dries to a blackboard finish and can be written on with chalk.

Colorizer: a concentrated color pigment used to tint white paint to a precise tone.

Colorwash: a mixture for colorwashing walls, made up of 50 percent wallpaper paste and 50 percent matte latex paint.

Cork tiles: flexible tiles made from cork, used for covering floors.

Cornice: a molding that runs around the join between a ceiling and wall. A cornice can also be "a decorative band of wood used to conceal curtain fixturess."

Curtain clip: a decorative clip used to attach fabric to a curtain pole.

Dado: a narrow wooden molding that runs along a wall at the height of the back of an upright chair.

Drop cloth: a tightly woven cotton sheet for covering furniture and floors before decorating.

Eggshell paint: an opaque, water- or oil-based paint with a low luster finish. Used on woodwork. This paint can be mixed to exactly match a matte latex paint.

Fleckstone paint: a spray paint that produces a granite-effect finish.

Floor paint: a tough paint for floors, designed to withstand heavy traffic.

Frosting film: a thin film that can be applied to glass to create a frosted effect.

Frosting spray: designed to be sprayed onto glass to create a frosted effect.

Gilt cream: a thick cream containing metallic particles. It can be rubbed onto a surface to produce a metallic effect.

Glass paint: a transparent paint designed especially for painting on glass.

Glass painting outliner: a thick substance used to draw the outlines of shapes on glass. The outlines can then be painted with glass paints.

Gloss roller: a small sponge roller used for applying gloss, satin, and eggshell paints. This can also be used with matte latex paint.

Grout: a substance for filling the gaps between ceramic tiles.

Grout float: a metal or plastic tool for applying grout. This can also be used on interior textured covering to create a rough plaster finish.

Grout stain: a pigment for coloring white or faded grout.

Hacksaw: a small saw for cutting metal and wood.

High gloss paint: an opaque, oil-based paint with a high luster finish. This can be used on woodwork in good condition.

High-density foam rubber: a strong, dense rubber for cutting stamps out of.

Interior textured covering: a thick, creamy substance that can be brushed onto a surface and then textured with a variety of tools.

Japan size: also known as gold size, this is used to stick metal leaf to a surface.

Joint compound: a flexible filler used for filling gaps and wide cracks in walls.

Laminate flooring: a faux wooden flooring with a particleboard substrate and a veneer or laminated top surface that imitates wood.

Laying off: the long, smooth brushstrokes used on the top coat of a brush-painted surface to diminish visible brush marks.

Lead strip: narrow strips of lead that are sticky on one side. This can be used for sticking onto windows to create a faux stained glass effect. It is available in different widths and in a brass finish.

Lining paper: thick, plain wallpaper used to cover a wall and smooth out the surface before painting it or hanging decorative wallpaper.

Long-pile roller: a painting roller with a soft, fluffy surface used for painting matte latex paint onto surfaces.

Masking: applying masking or painting tape to a surface to section, or mask off, an area to be painted.

Masking tape: paper tape for masking off when painting. This is available in various widths and degrees of stickiness.

Masonry paint: a tough, lightly textured paint developed for painting exterior surfaces. This can also be used in interiors.

Matte latex paint: an opaque, water-based paint with a completely matte finish. This can be used on walls and ceilings, and as an ingredient in color washes and pickling stains.

Melamine: a tough, easily cleaned surface material, usually used in kitchens.

Metal gauze: a fine metal mesh.

Metal leaf: very thin sheets of metal that can be stuck to a surface to produce a metallic effect. Usually available in gold, silver, aluminum, and various imitation and novelty finishes.

Metallic paint: a paint that imitates a metal finish. The higher the quantity of metallic pigment in the paint, the better the effect.

Mist coat: a primer for bare plaster, made up of 50 percent water and 50 percent matte latex paint.

Mitering: cutting a 45-degree angle in wood or another material.

Moldings: decorative wooden strips that run around a door or window.

Mosaic tiles: tiny tiles made from ceramic or vitreous glass.

Oil-based paint: a paint with a solvent base. It is more durable than water-based paint, but has a strong odor, can give off harmful vapors, and takes longer to dry.

Paint can: a small metal or plastic can for decanting paint into prior to use.

Paint effect: any decorative finish achieved with paint.

Paint thinners: a medium for diluting oil-based paint and for cleaning this paint off paintbrushes.

Painting tape: wide paper tape that has a low-tack sticky strip across half its width. Used to mask off sections of a wall for painting. This tape is particularly useful since the very low-tack glue does not lift paint off the wall when it is removed.

Phillips-head: screws with a locating cross in the top and screwdrivers with a corresponding cross at the point.

Pickling stain: a colored mixture of 50 percent matte latex paint and 50 per-cent water, used for tinting bare wood.

Primer: a coat of paint applied to a bare surface to prepare it for further painting. Specialist primers are available for some surfaces.

Project glue: a thick, very sticky adhesive used for fastening large or heavy items to various surfaces.

Sanding block: a specially designed block for wrapping sandpaper around to sand a rough surface flat.

Sanding sponge: a soft block covered with sandpaper for sanding walls and moldings.

Sandpaper: for smoothing wood and other surfaces. Available in various degrees of coarseness denoted by number. The higher the number, the finer the sandpaper.

Satin latex paint: an opaque, water-based paint with a medium luster finish. This can be used on walls that will need frequent wiping down.

Satin paint: an opaque, water- or oil-based paint with a medium luster finish. This can be used on woodwork. This paint can be mixed to exactly match a satin latex paint.

Scarf-in: to smooth two surfaces that are at different levels so that they become flush with one another.

Seaming roller: used to smooth the join between two drops of wallpaper once they have been hung.

Selvedge: the edge of the fabric that is formed in the weaving process.

Spackle: for filling holes and cracks in plaster and plasterboard walls.

Spirit level: a long metal or wooden rule that contains leveling bubbles. Used to determine whether a surface is level.

Spot filling: filling small holes or cracks in specific areas of a surface.

Squeegee: a rubber-edged tool for applying frosting film to glass.

Stippling brush: a paintbrush with stiff bristles that finish in a square or gently pointed tip. Used for creating paint effects and for stenciling.

Tieback: a decorative tie used to hold a drape away from a window.

Tongue-and-groove: narrow wooden boards that interlock. Used for covering floors and for cladding walls.

Top coat: the final coat of paint on a wall, or the second color in a paint effect.

Trompe l'oeil: a paint effect technique that makes a flat area look three-dimensional.

Try-square: a wooden or metal tool that contains a perfect right angle. Used to determine whether two surfaces are at right angles to one another, and to draw lines at right angles across a surface.

Varnish: a resinous, clear substance applied over dry paint, or a surface, to protect it.

Vinyl covering: thin, sticky-backed vinyl sheeting. This can be used to cover a variety of surfaces.

Vinyl tiles: flexible tiles for covering floors.

Voile: thin cotton fabric.

Water-based paint: a paint with an acrylic base. It is less durable than oil-based paint, however. Has less of an odor, is more environmentally friendly, and is quicker to dry.

Wide-gap grout: a special grout, usually in powder form, for filling wide gaps between ceramic tiles.

Wooden beading: a plain or decorative wooden molding.

SUPPLIERS

IN THE UNITED STATES

American Hardware Manufacturers Association
801 North Plaza Drive
Schaumburg, IL 60173-4977
Tel: (847) 605-1030
www.ahma.org

American Lighting Association
P.O. Box 420288
Dallas, TX 755342-0288
Toll-free: (800) 274-4484
www.americanlightingassoc.com

Briwax Woodcare Products
220 South Main Street
Auburn, ME 04210
Toll-free: (800) 274-9299
Fax: (212) 504-9550
www.BriwaxWoodcare.com
E-mail:
information@briwaxwoodcare.com

Do-It-Yourself Council
P.O. Box 1963
Columbus, IN 47201
Tel: (812) 376-9299
www.wdiyc.org

HK Holbein (Importers of Fine Artist and Designer Materials)
Box 555, 175 Commerce Street
Williston, VT 05495
Toll-free: (800) 682-6686
Tel: (802) 862-4573
Fax: (802) 658-5889
www.holbeinhk.com
E-mail: holbeinhk@aol.com

Kitchen Cabinet Manufacturers Association
1899 Preston White Drive
Reston, VA 20191-5435
Tel: (703) 264-1690
www.kcma.org

National Kitchen and Bath Association
687 Willow Grove Street
Hackettstown, NJ 07840
Tel: (800) 843-6522
Fax: (908) 852-1695
www.nkba.org

Paint and Decorating Retailers Association
403 Axminister Drive
St. Louis, MO 63026-2941
Tel: (636) 326-2636
Fax: (636) 326-1823
www.pdra.org
E-mail: info@pdra.org

Pearl Paints
308 Canal Street
New York, NY 10013
Toll-free: (800) 221-6845 x2297
Tel: (212) 431-7932 x2297
www.pearlpaint.com
E-mail: Pearlsite@aol.com

Pierre Finkelstein Institute of Decorative Painting, Inc.
20 West 20th Street, Suite 1009
New York, N Y 10011
Toll-free: (888) 328-9278
www.pfinkelstein.com
E-mail: pfinkel@earthlink.net

R&F Handmade Paints, Inc.
506 Broadway
Kingston, NY 12401
Toll-free: (800) 206-8088
Tel: (845) 331-3112
Fax: (845) 331-3242
www.rfpaints.com

IN CANADA

Sinopia Pigments & Materials
3385 Twenty-Second Street
(near Guerrero)
San Francisco, CA 94110
Tel: (415) 824-3180
Fax (415) 824-3280
www.sinopia.com
E-mail: pigments@sinopia.com

**Canadian Hardware and
Housewares Manufacturers
Association**
1335 Morningside Avenue
Suite 101
Scarborough, ON M1B 5M4
Tel: (416) 282-0022
www.chhma.ca

WEBSITES

www.bathweb.com
Website dedicated to bathroom
manufacturers, designers, and retailers.

www.closetweb.com
Website dedicated to closet
manufacturers, dealers, and designers.

www.kitchenweb.com
Website dedicated to kitchen design.

**Canadian Home Builder's
Association**
150 Laurier Avenue West
Suite 500
Ottawa, ON K1P 5J4
Tel: (613) 230-3060
www.chba.ca

**Canada Mortgage and Housing
Corporation (CMHC)**
700 Montreal Road
Ottawa, ON K1A 0P7
Tel: (613) 748-2000
TTY: (613) 748-2447
www.chba.ca/renovatingyourhome

INDEX

Acknowledgments

The author would like to thank Lucinda Symons and Brian Hatton for photography. Diana Civil for styling. Kate Haxell for everything else. Steve Gott for set building. Philip Haxell for technical help. Ben Dickens, Matt Dickens, Helen Burkinshaw, and Mr. and Mrs. Haxell for the loan of their homes. Giles Hall for canvas making and general management.

Photographic Acknowledgments:
46, 145, 165, 166; Tino Tedaldi; *Display* by Laurence Llewelyn-Bowen.
48, 138, 163; Tino Tedaldi; *Modern Paint Effects* by Annie Sloan.
77, 80, 82; Chrysalis Images; *The Floor Book* by Dominique Coughlin, projects by Sacha Cohen.
81; Tino Tedaldi; *Paint Alchemy* by Annie Sloan.
120; Peter Williams; *Wonderful Wire* by Mary Maguire.
134; Tino Tedaldi; *Sheer Style* by Tessa Evelegh.
150, 177; Simon Brown; *Spaces for Living* by Liz Bawens and Alexandra Campbell.
152; Lucinda Symons; *The Weekend Decorator*, by Amy Dawson and Gina Moore.